the Leadership Attitude

the Leadership Attitude

Inspiring Success
through Authenticity
and Passion

Deborah E. McGee

Advantage | Books

Published by Advantage, Charleston, South Carolina.
Member of Advantage Media.

ADVANTAGE is a registered trademark, and the Advantage colophon is a trademark of Advantage Media Group, Inc.

Printed in the United States of America.

10 9 8 7 6 5 4 3 2 1

ISBN: 979-8-89188-144-0 (Hardcover)
ISBN: 978-1-64225-715-1 (Paperback)
ISBN: 978-1-64225-714-4 (eBook)

Library of Congress Control Number: 2024902663

Cover design by Matthew Morse.
Layout design by Lance Buckley.

This publication is designed to provide accurate and authoritative information in regard to the subject matter covered. It is sold with the understanding that the publisher is not engaged in rendering legal, accounting, or other professional services. If legal advice or other expert assistance is required, the services of a competent professional person should be sought.

Advantage Media helps busy entrepreneurs, CEOs, and leaders write and publish a book to grow their business and become the authority in their field. Advantage authors comprise an exclusive community of industry professionals, idea-makers, and thought leaders. Do you have a book idea or manuscript for consideration? We would love to hear from you at **AdvantageMedia.com**.

To Mark: *Thank you for being my friend, confidant, husband, mentor, and father to our three sons. Your leadership and unique way of living your truth every day has been my inspiration. I thank God for bringing you into my life at such an early age, to walk beside me throughout this journey called life.*

Contents

Introduction

A few years ago, after thirty years in the fast-moving, hard-grinding corporate world, I found my calling. It came after I was downsized from an international position where I literally traveled and worked half of the time in another country, away from my family.

A CPA by profession, the downsize came when I was more than twenty years into a career in expatriate taxation and global human capital, the latter of which involves more than just the struggle with cultures and languages, but also complicates workplace communications. Global Human Capital Solutions is taking care of the most important assets in any industry, your talent. In today's world, post-COVID-19, our talent shortage is worse than ever, yet so many companies make the mistake of not embracing and taking care of their talent to ensure a great collaborative environment for them to work in. In a world where we "communicate" via the computer, sometimes with video and sometimes without, we have really lost the connective humanism that we need to feel a part of a group. We still need the human touch: We need to shake a hand, give a hug, have a meal together, and be in physical connection with each other to thrive in any industry. Now put that in an organization that spans across states and countries, timelines, cultures, and languages—that is truly what Global Human Capital Solutions is all about.

Interestingly, my husband was in the military while I was in my corporate career, and I used to joke about how easy it would have been to just quit my job and stay home raising our three sons rather than move around every two years and look for a new job. Make no mistake, I'm proud of the selfless career my husband chose to spend thirty-one years of his adult life in, but a military career is not a lone career as a business job is. Military is a culture that engulfs your family, your children, your living arrangements, and your faith. Research conducted by career website revealed a 30 percent divorce rate for enlisted first-line military supervisors. The research rated the position as the one with the greatest majority of divorces out of the twenty-one occupations studied.[1] I am fortunate (and yes it is a lot of work) that my husband and I have been married for forty-four years and raised three sons, and yet we still love—even like—each other.

When I was a young wife of six years (twenty-three years old), before we had our children, another senior spouse who was probably thirty years old and had two children gave me the best advice as a young military wife heading to Europe for the first time. "Don't wait for your husband to accompany you on trips," she said. "You'll never see anything, and you'll be resentful. If you have children, be prepared to raise them alone. It isn't an easy life, but it is a rewarding life." That was in 1984. I took it to heart, traveled Europe without him (often), fought hard to obtain my education, and started a career of my own. When the kids came along, I knew he would be there when he could but learned not to *expect* it. That may sound harsh and unrealistic for today's spouses, but it is simply the truth, and that advice at a very early adult age made me the independent woman and businessperson I am now *many* years later.

After twenty years of working with big global corporations wearing various hats, I realized I had not made time for myself and,

---

1   , "21 Careers That Are More Likely to Lead to Divorce," , accessed November 15, 2023, https:///news/21-careers-more-likely-lead-200001677.html.

more importantly, time for God. So after I thought I was done with my career, I instead founded my own company. Being a structured person, I immediately put in place a routine in my "retirement." I decided to answer the challenge by my pastor to read the Bible every day; it was something that I put off for a year, but it seemed the perfect time for me to take on some personal challenges. The more I read, the more my entire outlook began to change. The lessons I began learning about the different biblical warriors and leaders gave me insight and helped me begin to trust that God would put me on the path I needed to go—and he did. Great people started coming into my life—clients, employees, colleagues—and they all had one thing in common: they were believers in Christ and openly talked about it.

Today, my company, Group, is a family of seven entities that provide human capital solutions. We help organizations find solutions to their difficult problems, whether that is employment set up in a foreign country; how to deliver payroll in multiple currencies; domestic and international relocation solutions for employees and their families; management, analysis, and structuring difficult decisions from global employee information; international benefit solutions for a multinational workforce; or retaining and engaging their workforce in collaboration with the organization and fellow colleagues.

My goal with this book is to share insights on the human side of globalization and to equip formal and informal leaders with insights into a change in attitude to help them improve in their roles and their lives. My team and I at Group work with global corporations on these two elements: human capital and leadership attitudes. I also want to inspire readers to see how to put their Christian faith into capitalism and be successful. is a faith-based business, but no one needs to be a Christian to work here or work with us. We don't dictate to anyone how they should live their faith; that's between them and their God. But we are thankful for our opportunities, our employees, and our clients, and we pray routinely for the blessings we have and for divine guidance in our operations and decisions. We also prefer to align ourselves with people who have Christian values. That means we care about people, we put others before ourselves, and we're servant leaders. Those are the same values that people of many faiths, and even no faith, have.

When I started , I left behind a treadmill of corporate life that took me nowhere; it was filled with constant doubt and frustration, trying to prove I was good enough for the job, the promotion, the client, and the like. Jesus saved me from that constant doubt, and I didn't have to earn his acceptance; he accepts me as I am and only asks me to share his good news of what he did for me with others, to help others see that their ability and talent are from God who loves us and wants good things for us all.

This book is for leaders and entrepreneurs but especially for people who are informal leaders—those who have influence but not authority and how their leadership attitude is what really makes the difference in a good leader and a great leader. Most importantly, I want to reach out to corporate individuals who want to do well in the secular working world but would also like to be able to acknowledge their faith without fear of retribution.

I am not on the same path I envisioned when I was a young seventeen-year-old with visions of climbing the corporate ladder; ultimately, God had a much different plan, and it was one I couldn't have dreamed up, even if I had tried. There were people to meet, lessons to learn, and cultures to embrace before I would be ready to run an organization, as I am doing today. The one constant in my entire journey has been that I was willing to say, "Yes, I will go," even though I had no idea where, how, or if things would work out. I trusted God to lay the path; I just had to be courageous enough to take that path, much like Deborah, who in the book of Judges said, "Why me, Lord?" She had to learn to read the scribes, listen to God's voice in dealing justice and judgment, and lead people into the battle against impossible odds. For me, it has been about leading in business, but I believe my story and the lessons learned will resonate with people in many industries and fields, whether that's teaching, nonprofit, government, hospitality, healthcare, personal care, or whatever field you have been given talents for and have a passion ignited in you to do.

Chapter 1

When God Put Me in Time-Out

Blessed is the one who perseveres under trial because,
having stood the test, that person will receive the crown of
life that the Lord has promised to those who love him.

—JAMES 1:12 (NEW INTERNATIONAL VERSION)

For years, I'd felt that I was being told to go home, that I shouldn't follow the path I was on. It never felt right to me. But I kept putting it off until finally God said, "OK, I'll just take it away." And he did.

That time-out came just over two decades into my career in international management. It was the kind of job that many executives dream about—a high-powered, high-pressure position, with high-level paychecks. Like many high-level executives, I was totally dedicated to my career—I gave nothing less than 100 percent, seven days a week—and I had a long record of success and major job titles.

I worked at the Big Four global accounting firms in international executive management for thirteen years and at European and Asian companies in international human resources () for ten years. My job involved designing, developing, and implementing centers of excellence for large global organizations. Creating those centers is incredibly challenging, and daily struggles with many different cultures and languages can make communication difficult. But I worked extremely hard, did everything I could to learn my craft, and paid my dues. Remarking on one of the complete HR operations I implemented, one of my CEOs, the former head of , once told me that he had never known anyone who knew as much about as I did.

In my last corporate job, I was global head of for the largest division of a heavy equipment manufacturer in Asia, a company that had bought three divisions of heavy equipment makers in the United States in a $5 billion purchase as its US footprint.

The company hired me to design its entire function from the ground up; I took its decentralized HR—a messy and segregated process—and changed it to a centralized process. The division went from zero employees to sixteen individuals in four regions of the world: the Americas, Europe, Asia-Pacific, and China. During my time at this organization, I centralized all international management of global employees on various international assignments and centralized international travel with approval metrics and IT tools for the division. More than $50 million per year of internal spend budget flowed through my function within my division, and, all told, our division encompassed approximately fifteen thousand of forty-five thousand global employees operating in more than thirty countries.

A Hectic Schedule

Building such a massive division with so many international moving parts required me to spend more than 180 days each year in Asia, while my husband, Mark, and our three sons lived seven thousand miles away in the United States. I spent half of my time at the global headquarters in Korea and China and half of my time in the United States and in the company's European headquarters.

I landed the role after working for a French company while living in Washington, DC. At the time, my husband, Mark, was in the military and on duty in El Paso, Texas. For three years, while I worked in DC, where our home was, he worked out of El Paso, and we saw each other about every six weeks. Our three sons were also living apart: the oldest was in school at West Point, the youngest son was with Mark and going to school there, and the middle son was with me in DC and still in high school.

Since Mark was nearing retirement from the military at the time I took up the job in Asia, we were planning to move to Charlotte, North Carolina, where the company's US headquarters were located. Our sons would all be off to college by then, so it would just be the two of us. But before Mark's retirement was formalized, the company decided to move its US headquarters to Atlanta, Georgia. Mark did not want to live full-time in Atlanta, so we ultimately agreed on a home in , Alabama, just outside of Huntsville. It's a beautiful home on the lake, and its location would allow him to commute forty-five minutes to Huntsville once he returned to the corporate workforce after his military retirement, while I would commute three and a half hours to Atlanta and stay there for the workweek when I was in the States.

After we moved to Alabama, I would rise early on Monday morning and drive to Atlanta, where I stayed during the workweek in a rented apartment until Friday. On Friday morning, I would drive back home to and put in a full day of work and then spend the weekend with Mark. Every two weeks, however, I flew to Korea—a twelve-hour flight, with a fifteen-hour time difference—to work there for two weeks before flying back home to spend a weekend in and then commuting to Atlanta on Monday and spending the workweek there. That went on for more than three years.

While all the travel was hard on me physically and I felt some guilt being absent from family life so often, I was determined to pursue my career and prove my mettle within the organization. I thought the sacrifice of being away from those so close to me was worth the gain; the main priority in my life was being "successful" at work.

But Mark told me many times, "You're chasing something that will not leave you content and fulfilled, but I'm not tell you not to chase it. That's something you need to learn on your own."

On some level, I think he was probably right. I should have felt satisfied in such an exciting role, but deep down inside, it didn't feel right. I was raised in a solid Christian family. When I was young, I went to church on Sundays and Wednesdays and attended Sunday school classes. The principles of godly living were firmly planted in my heart. But as a busy executive in that role, I was expected to be away from family, and I often behaved in ways that were inconsistent with what I really believed in.

A Life-Changing Accident

Several years into my role with the organization, I was leaving Dubai after completing a business trip, about to board the plane back to Korea when I got a call from my husband.

"Where are you?" he said, sounding stressed.

"I'm at the airport in Dubai, and I'm about to catch a plane for Seoul," I said. "What's going on?"

"You might want to come home instead," he said. I'll never forget the worried sound of his voice. " fell twenty feet off a building and broke his back in three places."

At that time, our oldest son was already in the military and our youngest son was attending West Point, but , our middle son, was living with us in Alabama. Three years prior, he had received a scholarship to

University, where he promptly flunked out in his first year. However, instead of coming home to Alabama to go to school, he was determined to make it on his own, so he had gone to Virginia with some buddies to attend school there. Mark, who firmly believes in tough love, would not support the move. "You can come home," he had told , "but we're not paying for you to live in Virginia."

For those three years that was in Virginia, we were never sure what was going on with him; we often went months without hearing from him, and then we'd get a phone call asking for money for food or to get a place to live. Each time, Mark told him, "No, you can come home, and we'll even come get you, but we will not send you money."

Finally, after he had apparently exhausted all of his options, came home. He was twenty-one and still not ready to go back to school, but he got a steady job. However, he was drinking pretty heavily at the time, and he had taken to "roof jumping" as a sport. Often, there isn't anything you can do for your adult children but watch them make disastrous mistakes and learn from them. This was one of those times.

One night after he had been drinking, he was jumping from roof to roof (""), missed a step, and fell twenty-three feet to the concrete, bursting his , 2, and 3 vertebrae upon landing. It pains me to say it, but I thank God he was drunk when he fell because it made him limber.

"The doctors didn't know whether he'll be paralyzed or not," Mark told me on the phone. "They're preparing him for surgery." Mark had been at a meeting in DC and was on his way to the hospital in Alabama; thankfully, our son was lucid enough after the fall to have had the hospital call one of our friends, since neither one of us was in town when it happened, and they alerted Mark.

I quickly changed flights and started the arduous journey home, crying like a baby the whole way—it was the longest, most helpless fifteen hours of my life. For the entire flight, I kept thinking, "What am I doing on the other side of the world, working day and night? I don't need to be doing this—I need to be home with my family." It still chokes me up remembering the anxiety I felt as I sat there wondering the whole flight what shape my son would be in for the rest of his life—would he be paralyzed and unable to walk?

Mark made it home in time for the surgery, and God blessed us with fantastic doctors who were able to repair back. The doctors told us that our son "came within a fingernail" of severing his spinal cord because it didn't burst out, but it burst in. It was like a miracle—he walked out of the hospital three days later. He was in a head-to-waist brace for six months, and he would have to live with lifelong discomfort thereafter, but he would eventually be able to move and function normally. Today, he even does yoga and skis, but whenever it rains, he remembers his injury. The blessing is that his fall woke him up—three years later, he would finish college summa cum laude in three degrees: chemical engineering, chemistry, and mathematics. Today, he's a scientist, a virologist.

At the time, my son's situation gave me the same heartache any good mom would have, but it still wasn't enough to make me leave my job and stay home. As soon as he healed, I went back to work and was as laser-focused as ever. In my heart, I knew that my family had dodged a bullet, and this was a wake-up call, but I wasn't ready to give up my work yet.

Drastic Changes

As the company I worked for grew in the United States, corporate leadership decided it would be better if all executives in our division (the largest in the organization) were headquartered in Asia rather than the United States. This was a big change for the organization, and it sent panic throughout US operations. If our leadership wasn't on the same continent as we were, how would that affect us?

As part of the reorganization, the corporation went through an enterprise resource planning exercise, and each function was redesigned. My function not only dodged the redesign, but the organization also decided to take our program, systems, and processes and roll them out for the entire organization of forty-five thousand employees. That sounded like success, what I had been working hard for more than four years to achieve.

When I was called to a meeting at the organizational headquarters, I told my team that I would keep fighting for us so we wouldn't be redesigned—which could mean layoffs—but instead, we would manage the entire function for every division in the company.

I walked into the meeting thinking that's what we were there to discuss. I couldn't have been more mistaken.

The meeting took place at nine o'clock on a Monday morning. I expected to meet with the chief human resources officer, who was my boss, and the divisional headquarters vice president of HR. I was surprised to see the US vice president of HR there—that was unusual.

"Deb, as part of the reorganization, instead of you running globally, we want you to be responsible for only Europe and North America," the US vice president said.

"That means my function is no longer global?" I asked.

"That is correct," he said. "We'd like you to stay with the organization, but we don't need you to have sixteen team members across the globe. We want you to get rid of fourteen of them and keep two."

"So, my global position is going away, you want me to accept a demotion, and you want me to fire most of my team?" I asked. "No, that's not going to happen. Absolutely not. I won't do it."

"We thought that would be your answer," he said. "We're prepared to let you go, and we'll give you a severance package. We'd like you to stay for three months to help your team make the transition to a different manager."

I sat there, stunned and speechless. They had flown me seven thousand miles to fire me.

Where to Go from Here?

When I got back to the hotel, I broke down and cried—I was sad, hurt, and angry. I had designed and run an entire function for this organization. I had done all the hard work and utilized my intellectual capital, and I thought that would be appreciated. But clearly, they didn't value my contribution—I'm not sure they were even capable of that. After all, an organization is not people; it's an organization.

Like many executives who are let go because of a reorganization, I thought, "OK, I'll take some time and do all the personal things I always wanted to do but never had the time. This could be a good thing, right?"

After I thought about it, and if I'm honest, had a good little pity party, it made sense. I had been at the organization for five years and had grown it from nothing to where it was now. My team members were great and mature enough to stand on their own two feet and continue to move forward. So, I agreed to the deal to stay on for three months for the transition to the eastern head of the function, but I was not to tell my team that I was leaving the organization.

The eastern head who would replace me came to our North American headquarters for two weeks to understand what we had been doing and how to continue the work we had started. Instead, after a two-week period, he gave notice to corporate headquarters that he had to take a year sabbatical. He recognized he would not be successful in the role.

The company then asked me to stay on and run two regions, Europe and North America, but I turned the offer down—three times. I'm not a vindictive person, but I admit it was gratifying to see them realize the job I made look easy was actually very complex and difficult. They didn't understand that they had a valuable resource in me, and they didn't appreciate my contribution. Suddenly—and too late—they realized they made a huge mistake in letting me go.

I was confident that my team could continue on, if they chose to, but it was time for me to do something different. I wasn't sure what that was, but I knew that after spending five years separated from my husband and only seeing him about twice a month, it was time to stop and go home. God wanted me to take a time-out.

Should Have Heeded the Signs

Sometime later, I came to see my situation through the story of Nebuchadnezzar in Daniel 4:37. Here was a man who had defeated all the empires, destroyed Jerusalem, captured all the Jews, and tried to make himself a God in place of the true God. When God spoke to him and he realized the truth of his dreams, he still did not change his ways or heed God's warnings, so God carried out the punishment he said he would. God does not threaten; he warns us because he loves us. He is for us, not against us. But if we see the warnings and choose to ignore them, should the calamity that ensues surprise us?

When I was the corporate head, I thought I could change leadership's mind, and if I just worked harder and spent more time demanding change, it would happen. But God had a different plan for me, and even when I felt that, I ignored Him because I wasn't finished with my plan. The world, colleagues, coaches, and books all tell us: be bold, be assertive, keep going, and let nothing get in your way. What I missed is that it wasn't about me, but it was about what

I could do for my team, my employees, my friends, and my family. I wasn't bringing God into the picture at all. He had given me great opportunities and great resources, and I never gave him or anyone else much credit.

Thankfully, God didn't send me out into the wilderness to live like a beast for seven years, but he did give me a much-needed time-out. In corporate speak, it was "reorganization," a choice of firing my entire team, taking a smaller role within the organization, or being severed. I chose the severance. I listened; God was telling me to go home and take a break. My team would do fine without me, it was time for them to stand on their own feet, and I had to stop protecting them. Your team and your employees are not your children. They learn from corporate changes, just like we all learn from life changes.

The Next Chapter?

Regarding my work, I had no idea what I wanted to do next. I already had two great careers, and I moved up the corporate ladder both times. I was thirty years into my career and too senior—too costly—to fit into many corporate positions. The executive recruiter assigned to work with me as part of the organization's exit package made it clear: it would probably take two years to find a job that was as high-level and highly paid as the one I had.

I had a lot to offer any organization, and I was determined not to allow the situation to get the best of me. I pulled myself together, put my big girl panties on, and thought, "It's time to move forward—let's figure out what the next chapter of this life looks like."

At first, I was doing what I thought most retired people do, but the fact that I had no goal or direction made it an empty pursuit, a "placeholder" that kept me busy while I considered where my life was going.

I didn't know where to turn, so I went back to my Southern Baptist upbringing. When I was a kid, my dad read the Bible to us often, we attended church regularly, I went to Sunday school and church services on Wednesday nights, and I participated in church choir and youth group. For several years, the church Mark and I attended had been encouraging us to read the Bible over the course of a year. Even though we prayed to God, went to church, raised our children to believe in Jesus, and were faithful givers, it had been decades since I read the Bible daily, and I never really felt up to that point that I had a real *relationship* with God.

When I began to build that new habit of reading the Bible into my day, I decided to actually sit down and let God talk. I had always talked to him in the past, but this time, I began to listen.

Points to Ponder

1. In this new post-COVID-19 world of "life-work balance," do you feel that you can put your life events before your work events?

2. How do you make changes when your life expectations or interruptions cause you to be overlooked for important work projects or promotions?

3. Do you feel that your organization and the influencers around you are supporting you in achieving a good work-life balance? If not, how can you change that?

4. Whose responsibility is it to make changes in the culture of your organization, or do you just focus on your own work and personal life situation?

Chapter 2

That Was Then— the Pre-PZI Days

You make known to me the path of life; you will fill me with joy in your presence, with eternal pleasures at your right hand.

— PSALM 16:11 ()

W hen I began reading the Bible and listening to God, I began to change. I was happier and lighter, and things didn't bother me as much. People who ran into me after my career change, all said the same thing: "You've changed, you look great, and you seem really happy." I really wasn't ready to retire—I was only fifty years old—but I was happy to be out of the rat race.

When I was a woman in a man's world, I had always tried to prove that I was good enough. I had always thought if I worked harder, I would prove that I belonged at the top in the corporation.

In my last corporate role, I was one of the four female executives in an organization of forty-five thousand employees. Only one of those other females was Asian, and she was in charge of learning and development, a role that was OK to fill with a woman. The other two were running functions in an HR function.

The last few years of my time with the organization, it was going through an executive branding process where a number of men were put in high-level positions above me, but the Asian leaders of the organization refused to make my position high-level, even though it was approved by the position leveling committee. In that culture, my role was not considered qualified for a higher-level executive rank because they considered it a female position.

I've always found it interesting that, in Zechariah 5, "The Woman in a Basket," God used the vision of a woman in a basket as being "wicked and sin," yet she was also carried away by two other women with wings—so the abolition of that wickedness and sin was also carried out by women. Scholars often equate this passage to only evil being strong enough to deal with the evil woman in the basket; in other words, it took women to handle such a massive task. But all the time I was working in Asia, there were references to inferiority of my gender; for instance, sometimes suppliers did not believe that I was the author of certain policies—there was no way a woman was able to do such a thing.

Working in Asia—really anywhere outside of the United States— is different. In the United States, people work in cubicles or offices. We have more of our own personal space. In other countries, however, several people share desk space, and there's no partition between , no privacy, no personal space. It's like walking down a busy street in the United States or sitting in a busy restaurant; there are a lot of other people in an open space. When you arrive at work, there's no office to walk into, sit down, enjoy a great cup of coffee, or read your emails. You walk in and immediately you're in meetings, and you're taking notes. It's pretty much meeting after meeting, answering emails, making decisions—just go, go, go.

A Bulldozer, Not a Builder

Because I am such a driven person—a very Westernized driven person—instead of that open workspace making me more prone to building relationships, I was always looking to move the next thing forward. I was never an active listener, never really "touchy-"; instead, I just always said, "This is what we need to do," and then moved on. That's a very typical American thing to do, especially in American culture. Since then, I've had to learn to stop, take the time to listen, and look at what makes sense and how I can make a situation better. But that was not me back then.

At one point, my CEO had told me that what I was doing—creating centralization—was great and that it needed to be at the corporate level, not only just in our division. When I told him I didn't know how to get it to the corporate level, he told me, "You just keep going until I tell you to stop." So, I was the bulldozer. As a military spouse, if something doesn't exist, we create it. We know that nobody is going to give us anything, and they're not going to pay you for it either, so you just have to figure out what you want to do. That background was built into me at an early age, and it has served me both personally and professionally.

Eventually, my design, policies, and process did get rolled out to the entire organization, but while I was "just going until told to stop," I ended up alienating my Asian counterparts. My level of aggressiveness caused some male team members to lose face, and they hated me for it.

The Eastern way is to build relationships and build consensus as a team. No individual group is more important; your division is part of a whole. There is no individual success, because that means everyone else fails, and so the whole organization fails. That took me some time to really understand. Getting consensus before moving forward was such a foreign concept for Western organizations and executives to understand that, in five years' time, I had five different bosses (chief HR officers), and the company went through six CEOs, three , and three . In the West, we see an opportunity, we take it, even if it isn't well thought out, even if we have no idea how we're going to do it or know whether we really can do it. Our answer is, "Of course, we can do it," and then we figure it out.

Once I had caused my counterparts to lose face, they couldn't allow me to succeed because it would've looked even worse on them. One young, male manager who worked for me was actually pulled aside and told by a vice president that working for me would mean the end of his career. (To this day, that young man still contacts me to say thanks for all that I did for him.) Fortunately, the American HR chief whom I reported to would not allow anything to happen to me, but the male Asians were serious about proving that I couldn't be a leader. For instance, in most organizations, as a global head of operations, when it's time to roll out a policy, you typically get C-suite approval. Not in that organization. Even if the CEO gave the green light to something I had done, it did not mean I had the authority to do it because full consensus across all divisions was not obtained before the CEO gave his blessing. As a female, I was not going to get consensus in all divisions of that organization. That went on for the last three years of my role at that organization.

Big Responsibilities

Still, I loved managing expatriates; these were individuals who were employed in one country and being sent to another country to work. I did not manage their job; my team and I managed their life situation, all the things that are not work related: family assistance, shipment of clothing and household goods, where to live, how to get around, where the kids go to school, finding a , speaking the language, how to behave in a different culture, where to go for healthcare, getting paid, and then paying taxes. All those behavioral, situational pieces of a successful international assignment is what an person is responsible for. All the day-to-day things that support us in our work environment that we just take for granted when we live in the United States, those are the responsibilities of the HR global mobility group.

That may be one reason people in the global HR industry often struggle. They understand that HR is about inputting data into a system and making sure that the personally identifiable information () is protected and that people are getting paid. They understand what it means to perform an HR role, have tools to do their job with, and that when an employee leaves work for the day, their HR job is done—they don't care about where the person lives, or what they eat, or where the kids go to school. That's not part of their job description. But in an international situation, all of what happens outside the workplace is the HR professional's problem.

In my last role, I had a team of sixteen people reporting to me from four locations—Seoul, Belgium, Beijing, and Atlanta—and we managed around three thousand people, the majority of whom were international assignees from all over the world. Since I had centralized all of the functions in one department, the cost for all those services—$50 million per year—came through my department.

Those expenses included things like vacation time, which in global HR is called "home leave." When an international worker goes on vacation, they go back to their home location. Although it's called home leave, it's really a way to keep track of talent to ensure they don't go anywhere else while they're out of your sight. They come back once every six months or a year for a face-to-face meeting and to reconnect, which allows the company to maintain that relationship so that their investment doesn't walk off to their competitor. There are taxation issues involved too. These are things that executives at higher levels often don't realize the value of because they're not thinking about the supervisor who is going to lose that talent.

"Learn How to Drink and Sing"

After a few years of being laser-focused, aggressively moving things forward, and alienating my coworkers, my direct supervisor, the chief human resources officer, called me when I was at home in the United States and said, "Debbie, I want you to come to Asia for two weeks. I don't want you to have any meetings. I don't want you to move any agenda forward. I want you to get to know your colleagues. I want you to learn how to drink and how to sing karaoke."

After that, my Asian colleagues encouraged me to go out after work every day, drink heavily, sing karaoke loudly, and use language that would make a sailor blush. It was simply part of their way of doing business.

I was uneasy about the situation—drinking, staying out late, and using bad language went against my Christian background—but I was singularly focused on moving up the corporate ladder, so I went right along with it. I had no choice. It might as well have been part of my job description. In that organization, as in my others, there was no in-between—either you're all in or you're out.

During a global HR meeting, the company had a big social affair for the HR groups—forty people from all the teams attended, including the team I led. Toasting and drinking were a main part of the event. One by one, everyone stood up, poured drinks, and gave a toast. As the head of my function, I was responsible for my team and ensured that we went right along so that we looked good to the other groups.

The CEO of the organization sat across from me, and after about twenty minutes of toasting and drinking, he came over to me and said, "Debbie, you drink well!" That wasn't exactly the compliment I wanted to receive from the CEO. I wanted him to compliment me on working hard and getting great results, the things I had focused on and devoted so much of my life to.

24

Ultimately, the hard-driving, stressful lifestyle took its toll. All the alcohol, lack of sleep, eating all the wrong things, and overeating when I did have time to eat—all the bad habits they tell you not to do, that was me. I did every one of them. As a result, I was 120 pounds overweight and prediabetic, had high blood pressure, and felt exhausted most of the time. At 240 pounds, I was just "that close" to needing a seat belt extender on an airplane. (Today, I can sit in the middle seat, no problem.)

A Fresh Start

When the company let me go, I began thinking about taking a few months to relax and decompress. I admit I felt hurt that there had been a plan to get rid of me, something that had been considered for some time. With so many thoughts running through my head, I needed time to sort them out.

After I flew home to the United States, I moved everything from the corporate apartment in Atlanta back home to , Alabama, to live with Mark in our home, a beautiful place right beside a lake. I had lived apart from Mark for so long that I joked, "We'll give this living together thing a shot, but if it feels claustrophobic, I might have to get my own place."

Even though my husband and I had spent so many years apart, what kept us strong was that, no matter where we were in the world, we made sure that God was always in the marriage. We met as teenagers, went to church together, and were married in a church, so we made Christian vows to each other. While we were both raised in the church and were Christians, I wouldn't say we were strong in our faith. Still, with every move we made over the years, we always found a church to attend, even if it wasn't one that we were entirely comfortable in. We joke about it now that going to church was our weekly car wash; we just needed to go get our souls cleaned as a way to start over again.

Mark and I have always been a team. He has been my best friend since we were teens, and he's always been honest with me, sometimes even when I wish he wouldn't. He tells me what nobody else would dare tell me. To others, it may look like we're arguing sometimes, but that's not the way we see it; we're debating. We're not angry, but we're both type A personalities. We're not embarrassed to pray in front of others before a meal, and as a couple, we've always been involved in some kind of small group at church. We don't really pray together when we're talking long distance, but we end every single conversation by saying, "I love you."

To this day, we hold hands in church, and we both feel that God is with us all the time. When I see other parents in church who are sitting apart with their children between them, I tell them they should sit together because that's what brought their children into the world. The children should not come between them; instead, the parents should be a team. We love our children, but kids can destroy a marriage. We see marriages fall apart because of the children or because of money; those two things will absolutely destroy a marriage.

While I thought Mark and I would be together more once I returned to Alabama, he had retired from the military at that point and was working for a government contractor. He didn't deploy to war zones anymore, but he worked twelve hours a day, spending hours on the phone when he wasn't on-site. So much for spending quality time together.

Time to "Detox"

I found out it takes time to "detox" from corporate life, where I was connected 24/7 to my cell phone and computer, juggling clients in many different time zones. Once I was away from that, I began to feel withdrawal symptoms. Now and then, I desperately opened my laptop to see if someone I used to work with reached out to me, for any reason. I missed those connections. I knew if I didn't develop some sort of daily routine, I'd be an emotional wreck.

So, right after I moved home, I began waking up at eight o'clock, reading my Bible, and writing down my prayers in a journal. Then I'd go to the gym, and, before long, I was putting the same energy into working out every day that I used to put into working. I'd start with , do some , and then move on to classes, yoga classes, and spin classes—sometimes all in the same day. I'd stay there until around noon, and then I'd come home and piddle around for a few hours. During that detox time, I enrolled in master gardening classes, ballroom dance classes, and gourmet cooking classes, and on weekends, I created elaborate meals for Mark, and we enjoyed that time together. After twenty-five years on the corporate treadmill, I really needed that downtime.

After about six months, though, I really began missing my professional life. I had worked at my career for twenty-five years and really was lost without it. I initially thought about becoming a instructor because I really enjoyed it and was good at it. But a friend suggested that I think about getting back into business.

Do I Really Want a Job?

At that point, I had no idea where my career would go next—as a matter of fact, I didn't know whether I wanted a job or not—but the Lord started putting inspiring people in my path.

I attended a few meetings of the Society of Human Resource Management () and International Trade Association (ITA), simply because I wanted to put on a business suit—the "uniform" I wore for so many years—and have lunch with professional people. I met some spectacular women at those meetings—many were strong Christians—and they gave me ideas of what I might do next, including connecting with recruiters to search for job opportunities. I figured that while I looked around, I'd get to know my "new city" and think deeply about my new circumstances.

I knew reinventing myself would be difficult, but I wasn't afraid of it. After all, as a military spouse of thirty-one years and twenty-two moves of our family from one city to another, I was used to starting over. In the past, I always landed in a military community, a circle of people with whom I had something in common. This time, I didn't have that comfort zone—I was starting from scratch.

I met with a recruiter, and she wasn't encouraging: "Deb, with your experience and previous compensation that included pension, long-term incentive plans, and bonuses, it could be two years before you find a job at your level." I thought she was exaggerating. Maybe she didn't understand the work I did and didn't know how to find the right position for me.

A Different Kind of Interview

She wasn't the only one who didn't understand. When I applied for a job as a compensation and benefits manager at a large organization in our area, the manager who interviewed me wasn't sure how to conduct the interview.

She started with the usual questions, such as, "Where do you want to be in five years?" "What are your strengths and weaknesses?" and "Can you give me an example of a difficult problem that you were able to find a solution for?"

My answers must have been very different from those she was used to hearing. The interview turned into more of a conversation, and

I gave her advice on how she could create strategies in her company that would help it grow, not exactly what she was used to hearing from job candidates.

"On your website, it says that your company is in sixty countries," I said. "How do you manage the compensation benefits function in those countries?"

"I don't know," she said. "I'm not sure how we're doing all of that."

"Let's talk about that," I said. "It's important that your company focuses on growing your HR function so you have sufficient resources in every country. How are you growing HR?"

"Honestly, I don't know," she said.

"OK, let me give you some ideas," I said. I took her through the essential steps for growing HR to meet the needs of a global workforce. That's how the "interview" ended, with me helping her better understand her job. It certainly wasn't the kind of interview I expected—I didn't get a job from it—but it felt good to share my expertise.

Nothing to Lose

When I didn't hear back from the organization, I realized that the idea of working within a domestic group wasn't really my destiny. I would always be someone who was looking to advance the plan, the blueprint, and the international possibilities of what a function, an organization, could do. It was part of my professional DNA.

If I started my own business, I'd be totally on my own: my money, my time, my intellectual capital—and my courage. Where would I even begin? I couldn't compete with the large organizations; I was a one-woman show, no matter how much I knew.

But people had encouraged me to go out on my own. The treasurer for my former organization said that since I was managing

$50 million a year, I knew what was valuable and where all the money should go—that's a big reason I should start my own business.

A good friend of mine in that company was Dusty, who was responsible for the organization's capital spending. My budgets and my expenses had to go through his department in the finance division. He taught me a lot about cash flow and the importance of it, when to spend and when to finance, and what was acceptable debt and what was not. I spent many an early morning in his office, before the rest of the staff would arrive, talking about how my team would be managed after I left, and a little bit of motherly "look after them when I'm gone."

Dusty told me I should consider opening up my own company. I laughed at him—how would I even start something like that? I didn't know how to get clients in a new city to trust me, and I would be competing against the big consulting firms. He patiently explained that I had more knowledge of my specialty than anyone he had ever seen in his more than thirty years of corporate finance.

It would be up to me to recreate myself, and, since it can take years for the money to start coming in with most entrepreneurial ventures, my husband, Mark, wasn't convinced that new path was right—to him, it seemed like a lot of work and not a lot of income. Wouldn't it be easier to get a domestic job and fit back into the seams of a new organization?

That was not what I was reading in my Bible: to be bold, to be a warrior, to take chances and follow a new path that God was laying out. If I was going to start my own company, I would need the strength from God that was leading me to it. I decided to obey his will and give it a shot. Let's see where it goes—I had nothing to lose and everything to gain.

Points to Ponder

1. Is there something holding you back from finding your best self? What is it, and how can you get around it?

2. What relationships mean the most to you, and how are you keeping them strong?

3. Fear is a powerful tool of Satan. Is he utilizing the fear of failure over you to ensure you stay where you are and don't venture out into a new path that God may be laying out for you?

Chapter 3

When Faith Found Its Way In

"So now, go. I am sending you to Pharaoh to bring my people the Israelites out of Egypt." But Moses said to God, "Who am I that I should go to Pharaoh and bring the Israelites out of Egypt?" And God said, "I will be with you. And this will be the sign to you that it is I who have sent you."

—EXODUS 3:10–

When I went home and started reading the Bible, and actually listening to God's Word, I began to realize how having God and faith in my life provides foundational values and structure.

I've always been a structured person, and when I was severed, I knew I needed a routine. Per the instructions of the Bible book plan that our pastor had shared, every day, I read two chapters in the Old Testament and then one chapter in the New Testament. Our church pastor had told me, "If you don't know what to look for in the Bible, just open it, and God will take you to the perfect place for your situation." But I wanted to be methodical in my study of the Bible. I figured that if I was starting a new chapter in my life, why not start at the beginning of God's Word, and as I read, I'd see where he led me?

As I read through the Bible, my thinking became clearer, and I observed signs happening around me. By actively listening to and for his voice, I began to get direction from God instead of just randomly going from one activity to another.

I kept reading over and over, especially in the Old Testament, about people who had extreme adversity thrown at them and wanted to give up. Then they cried out to God, and things happened: something came about, someone came into their life, something changed. Reading those stories made me realize that God is still doing the same things, and he'll do them for anyone, if they just ask.

Be the Deborah

I found myself especially drawn to the passages about Deborah, a female leader and adviser, known then as a "judge," of Israel. Deborah, which means "little bees," could deliver a "sting" with her words, when needed. She was often called upon to settle disputes and give advice. In Judges 4:5, she is shown as sitting under a palm tree, listening to the Word of God. There, people in need of advice would come to her for judgment on what to do about their situation, and she would pass on the messages heard from God.

One of those messages helped make her a national heroine to the Israelites. In Judges 4:1–16, 5:1–23, when the neighboring Canaanites, who were ruled by King of, waged war on the Israelites, Deborah rallied the troops, even though they were vastly by army. She also taunted men to pursue battle onto the ground that, when dry, would hold the army's thundering chariots. But just before the battle, a great downpour came and turned the ground to mud. There, the hundreds of Canaanite chariots bogged down, giving the Israelites the advantage—and win. Deborah had listened to God and trusted in him, and right won out over might.

Deborah stands out for her wisdom, courage, and faith, and through her story, I began to realize that it was time for me to stand up and speak out of my experiences in God. When I think of her, in her time being one of the judges of Israel, where men and women, rulers and slaves all listened to her and did as they were instructed, it gives me the courage that, with Jesus front and center, there isn't anything I can't do. In business, life, different cultures, and when facing the impossible, I have seen again and again women lead the crusade. The more I read, the more I saw parallels in my own life, and the more I began to believe that I—and all women—must "Be the Deborah." As a Christian woman of God who has been blessed again and again, I began to feel that it was time for me—for all of us—to bring the counselors, the prophets, the intellect on this journey. As women of God, raised to show the fallen world God's love, mercy, miracles, and the path he has for us, we need to quit making it so hard on ourselves. We don't have to do it alone. If we love and obey our Father, he will provide for us.

Combating Adversity

When I was in the Word, I was quiet, both physically and mentally. The constant chatter I used to have in my head from years of waking up at two o'clock at night, answering emails 24/7, taking phone calls, and struggling to meet impossible deadlines was gone. The more I was available for God, the closer I felt to him, which isn't surprising—James 4:8 tells us, "Draw closer to God and he will draw closer to you."

I wasn't just reading, I was really starting to study, and it was starting to sink in. I had always been the kind of parent who would say, "Jesus, give me patience," or "Lord, help me get through this." But those were not really prayers in earnest. This time, I began writing my prayers down in a journal—my "Journal to Jesus." When I started consciously praying, I formalized that process too. I would start each prayer with thanks for all the ways I've been blessed, and then I prayed for focus, strength, and courage. I also prayed for clarity because I needed encouragement and discernment since I had pretty much lost my way—something I'm sure many executives feel at some point in their career. I have since gone back and read those prayers, and it is amazing to see how many have been answered.

Reading the Bible and all those stories started to calm me. I read story after story—Abraham, Isaac, Joseph, Moses—the list went on and on. When the Lord requested that they do something very difficult, they all responded in the same way: "Are you kidding me? I can't do that!"

Eventually, they all listened, took that leap into the deep end of the pool, and didn't drown, because God had them. I wanted to believe that God had me too. I started to personalize every story in the Bible. How must those people have felt? Scared. Anxious. Alone. Bewildered. Those feelings applied to me too, and the Bible stories made me feel better, simply because those great characters, those people whom the Lord cherished, felt the same turbulent emotions that I did.

I began to see parallels in what I was dealing with, and I began to get clarity about my own situation. I was in a new town. I didn't really know anybody. I didn't have any connections there. I knew I was a good consultant, but no one in this city knew me or even knew my industry. I didn't have my business world around me. I just needed to go out and meet some people. I joke that I just wanted to put on my business suit and go to lunch with other businesspeople; I just wanted to talk to someone about business. It took me a while to figure that out, and reading through the Bible gave me the courage to begin.

Taking the Opportunities

God gives us opportunities every single day; we have to be discerning enough to recognize them and take a chance on them. My job had always been to build a foundation and have the knowledge and good facts in order to be able to take those opportunities when they came. Now I needed to get better at recognizing that the opportunities came from God and that he was working through me.

Today, my company, (People Zealously Interconnected), is about providing God's people the foundation for having the job they enjoy. I originally named the company based on the first initials of my three sons' names: Patrick, Zachary, and Ian. People tried to discourage me from using the initials, but I had worked for several big firms that were known by their initials, so I thought, why not? However, the initials left people asking about what they stood for. Then, when I brought Michelle Nash into the company as director of outreach relations and to help market the company, she told me, "Debbie, I can't market Patrick Zachary Ian." So, she came up with the name, "People Zealously Interconnected."

At first, I didn't care for it, but then I thought, "OK, Jesus is zealous for us, and I'm zealous for giving people that foundation." We're a company made up of primarily military spouses and veterans, we're passionate about that, and "passionate" is another word for zealous. We're all about people, we put people first, so that part made sense. The "interconnected" part—having close relationships with our customers and employees—is vitally important to everything we do. So, People Zealously Interconnected it is.

At , we take care of people, and that's what Jesus did. He took care of people. That's why our foundation is Christian values. We're good at what we do because we know our trade, but God gave us the brains to be able to do our jobs well, and I believe he gave me a brain for leadership and entrepreneurship. Still, I want to give him the glory for it all because I truly believe that's where our success comes from. He has given us opportunities that we might not have otherwise had.

It just took time for me to become conscious of where the opportunities are really coming from and realize that he is at the wheel. Often, we get so wrapped up in thinking we can control things; if we just calm down and let things happen, we can begin to see those opportunities. It's really about retraining yourself, especially in a world of "Be better," "It's all about you," "Take control of your career," and "You're responsible for yourself." Well, not really—it's all him. When we're younger, we focus so much on ourselves, and we're blind to everything around us because we believe that we make things happen. But as we get older and we've had more life experience, we see so much, we start to realize that there's no way we're in this solo.

The Courage to Connect as a Christian

Can it be OK to be a Christian in today's world and the corporate environment? Can we create a work environment where it's OK to speak your mind without fear of stepping on someone else? It takes a lot of courage and determination, and you may lose clients or employees, but maybe they weren't a good fit anyway. God never said it was going to be easy to be a Christian, and it comes with persecution. You cannot be afraid to speak your truth. Don't be afraid to let God in.

When I was young, if something needed to be done, I'd figure a way out to do it. People who have that skill set tend to naturally gravitate to my company because we do allow them to have that ability to learn. There are borders to work within, but at , they have a strong foundation to build on and let God guide them where to go; that has attracted some truly wonderful, strong Christians into the organization.

In the corporations I used to work for, talking openly about Christ was not encouraged; it was not OK. Granted, I live in the Bible

Belt now, but what surprised me when I started going to business events was that prayers are something people still do here in Alabama. It's OK when we're talking about something and someone says, "It's a God thing," or "Thank God for that," or "I couldn't have done it without Jesus." It's not just slang; they mean what they say.

Similarly, I've often heard clients share their faith. We'll be talking about something, and they will say something like, "We wouldn't be where we are if it wasn't for the good Lord" or "Our prayers have come true." Or sometimes I might say something like, "I've been praying about it," and they'll quickly answer, "So have we." As soon as God enters the conversation, other people start opening up, and amazing things start happening.

Make no mistake: no one has to be a Christian to work here. As a faith-based company, what we're really saying is that those are our values: we take care of other people first, we're servant leaders, we care about people, and we care about one another. So, while being Christian is not part of any job description, people who work here must have what we view as Christian values. They must demonstrate in their actions and words that they know what it means to make sure that they do their best for others. That's what we expect.

In other words, we live the Gospel out loud; often that is "through the back door" but not in an overt way. For example, when we meet with clients or a partner company, we bring the Gospel to them not only by treating them as we want to be treated (golden rule concept) but also by treating them as *they need* to be treated—we meet them where they're at.

Michelle has grown from director of outreach relations to our vice president of human resources and workforce development. She explains it this way:

> Often, I'll mention in a client meeting that we're a Christian company without actually saying that. I'll say something like, "Being a woman of faith and working for a company made up of people who are strong believers, this is something we strive for." I don't say what we believe, and at that moment, someone will say, "I could tell that you're a believer." Someone else will say, "I appreciate that because I'm a believer too," and another person will add, "I've been a believer for most of my life." The connection that forms at that moment happens because of the common thread of faith, and it's very powerful.

At times, we also have prayer in the workplace. When we have our "non-meeting monthly meetings," staff minutes, a town hall, or a luncheon, I usually pray beforehand. I think it's important to thank God not only for the opportunity he brings us and the people he brings us to do those opportunities with but also to thank him for our food and other things that we have. We're a more remote workforce now, but when we have video meetings—and let me just say, I'm amazed to see how many are on the call these days (forty-one at last count!)—I start with a prayer because if I really want my truth to be told, I have to start with my own employees.

Making the Christian connection in the workplace wasn't something that started right away. I was always very private with my faith and didn't want to "intrude" my beliefs on someone else. But as I began to grow in my faith, I became bolder in saying things like, "God willing," "Only by the grace of the Lord," and I would get phrases similar in return. It was really surprising to find out how many people were just showing up and talking openly about Christ, whether it was a client or an employee. In business meetings with new people or in new organizations, I would find people who believed as I did and weren't afraid to talk about it. Sometimes when I open the door just a little bit, the flood comes through.

Since I saw Jesus working so obviously in my life, I ultimately couldn't keep it quiet. I asked my small group at church to pray for me to learn to pray out loud. It wasn't comfortable at first, and I even would write down what I wanted to say because I always got a bit tongue-tied when all eyes and ears were on me. I recalled how a woman whom I worked with would very briefly bow her head before a corporate meal, and I knew she was praying but never had the courage to ask her if I could join in. So, I started by taking the initiative to occasionally say, "Do you mind if I just say a quick prayer?" Most people are fine with that.

What I've found since is that prayers are all-encompassing. It doesn't matter what faith you practice. In the military, there are many different faiths—Christian, Muslim, Jewish, Hindu, Buddhism—and chaplains have to learn to lead prayers in a way that speaks to everyone. I never want to say that my faith is better than anyone else's faith. We all say prayers of thanks, we all pray for the best to happen, and we all want to give credit when an opportunity comes our way.

Today, when people come into my office just to tell me about a new opportunity that came to , I remind them that God is good to us every day. For instance, we had one employee in the finance department who was really great at his job, but he was an atheist. One day he came into my office to tell me about a phone call he had just received to let me know that a huge amount of money was about to come in, to which I said, "It's just a God thing. I mean, do you really think we're that good?" He just chuckled, slowly shook his head, and went back to work.

Coming Out of Retirement

When I first started thinking about starting my own consulting business, I was determined it would be one where people come first. I reached out to some of my former colleagues to let them know what I was up to: I was "coming out of retirement" and would be available to help them with any consulting type of projects they might need. When leaving an organization, it's important not to go dark, at least not for too long. If you want to stay in touch, you might be the one who has to do it. To this day, I am still very connected to those people, grateful to them for taking a chance on me and for helping me get my confidence back as a subject matter expert.

I also asked Jesus to use the Holy Spirit to talk through me, to use my abilities to show the world his love and caring and be the best steward for his business that I could be. It's also been helpful to have strong Christians on my team; they have believed in me and helped me to grow, and their strength has given me the strength to stand out in front.

Finally, as a military spouse with twenty-two moves under her belt, I had reinvented myself many times. This would just be one more thing, right? Well, I found out that getting a job and trying to start a business are two very different things.

I'll be honest, there was part of me that thought, "What if I fail at this?" I felt like a fish out of water. I was a high-level subject matter expert in my chosen field, but that didn't mean I'd be a successful entrepreneur or a good leader. Actually, I knew I wasn't a good leader. When I was in corporate life, I pressured my team to succeed way too much, mainly because of the pressure I was getting from the top. Because I was so focused on results, I didn't spend time caring about my people, developing them and helping them get to the next level. When I look back on it, I realize that I couldn't see past my day-to-day grind and help my team realize they didn't need to prove anything to me—I hired them because I believed in them. Unfortunately, I didn't tell them that very often. If I wanted to have a successful business with a productive, fulfilled team of employees, I had to do it differently this time.

A Place of Business

When you start out as an entrepreneur, you quickly find out nothing is handed to you—you have to make all the effort yourself. I reached out and joined a group of wonderful, strong female CEOs in Huntsville called "Girls Just Having Lunch" (they had that name so that they could put it on their business calendars and no one would know where they were). Several of them directed me to bankers, accountants, and lawyers and told me which organizations in town would be best for me to join to build relationships.

One of the best pieces of advice I received was about establishing a place of business. At one of our luncheons, I asked the group, "When do you know it's time to move into an office and stop meeting your clients at Starbucks?" Everyone laughed because they all started out exactly the same way.

After the luncheon, the CEO of the Women's Business Center in northern Alabama took me aside and told me she was moving her organization into a place called the Entrepreneur Incubator. She asked if I would consider taking a small office there. I made what was a big move for me at the time—I rented a small office for $325 a month. There, I met the CEO of a well-known and successful for-profit organization, who was the most openly Christian person I've ever met in a business setting. She had a huge cross in her office, and whenever I would talk to her about something, she'd interject into the conversation a phrase like, "Praise God" or "Isn't God great?" It was routine for her, and yet she received the Business of the Year award numerous times, and all her employees loved her because she was always true to herself. She was such an inspiration to me; she showed me that it's OK to be a Christian in the workplace, and if people don't like it, they don't have to work for you. There are other places they can work.

Still, $325 per month seemed to be a huge investment. I had only a few clients and no staff—should I be spending that money? Couldn't I just continue working out of my home and meeting clients at their office? But I stuck with my commitment to have a place of business and managed to pay the rent every month on time.

Making a Difference

My husband, Mark, didn't understand why I was starting a company instead of just getting another job. To him, starting a business seemed like a ton of work with no payoff any time in the near future.

He always felt that work was just a job, and it didn't give him the type of fulfillment that I was looking for, so why would I do this? He was putting in a lot of hours for a big government contractor and making a long drive every day, so the idea of me driving forty-five minutes to my Huntsville office just didn't make sense to him. He knew it was a tough lifestyle to maintain. It would take years for Mark—who is a believer—to truly understand that starting my business wasn't about me but rather something that I was being called to do.

I don't know a successful entrepreneur who started their business because they wanted to make a lot of money. They do it because they have a passion for something, or they want a better work-life balance than they had before, or they want to make a difference. Those all described me, so I was trusting in the Lord to help me do what he wanted me to do.

Points to Ponder

1. Think back on things that you've prayed for; how many of your prayers have been answered?

2. Think about how you pray. Do you simply say thanks? Are most of your prayers asking for something material? Now think about how you might alter those prayers to something more conceptual—strength, endurance, courage—and then consider formalizing your prayers with a "Journal to Jesus."

3. If you are in a situation that is not a faith-based workplace, how can you be the first to open that door?

Chapter 4

From Nothing to Something

> *But if we walk in the light, as he is in the light, we have fellowship with one another, and the blood of Jesus, his Son, purifies us from all sin.*
>
> — 1 JOHN 1:7

When I first started out, I just thought maybe I would do some occasional consulting-type work, which so many executives do when they retire. I have always enjoyed helping people find "that answer" that they are looking for; so many times, clients would tell me, "We've spent months looking at this problem, and within fifteen minutes you've told us exactly how we can accomplish this with your help."

As I started to reach out to possible clients, I felt frustrated—I couldn't get my "pitch" right. My business was complex, and no one had ever done anything like it—a complete outsourcing model in which the main focus was delivering employee satisfaction.

I knew what my internal business customers thought of me, the satisfaction they had because of what I had done for them. I wanted to bring the same thing to my new clients, but I had trouble communicating exactly what I did.

Then I had an idea: Why not reach out to some of my former colleagues and let them know what I was up to? I contacted a number of them and told them I was coming out of "retirement" and I'd be available to help them with consulting projects. As a young accountant in the , I was taught very early that if you wanted to work, you would be expected to find clients. So, I pulled some of those past skills out of the closet and dusted them off. Granted I didn't have the big consulting firm's names on my business card or large corporation backing me, but I did still have the intellectual capital I had acquired over the past twenty years and the ability to listen to what people needed, to find a solution and present them an offer.

A few of those former colleagues got back to me, asking for help with their specific needs, and I delivered. Even though I knew those people from working with them years ago, I considered them new clients—a good step forward for my fledgling business and for me personally.

The First Big Client

To build a base of contacts—and ultimately, clients—I attended regular meetings with the Society of Human Resource Management () and International Trade Association (ITA). I also became involved in the North Alabama International Trade Association () and the National Foreign Trade Council (), knowing I'd need to join other organizations to meet new contacts.

At one of the North Alabama luncheons, I sat down at a table with a woman who happened to be the sitting manager of HR for a local automotive manufacturer in the area. She and I started talking, and when I told her what I used to do before "retirement," she told me she was having issues with sending someone to another country. We met later to discuss her problem more in depth. I listened as she presented the details, and within a few minutes, sirens started going off in my head. I was dying to blurt out, "Stop, you don't want to do that!" and "That's not the right solution!" but I calmly waited for her to finish and told her I'd love to help her solve the problem.

It felt good to be in that position again—using my years of experience to recognize the flaws in a plan and present better options. That was the first client at , and we still do business with them. When my original contact left for another opportunity, she brought me in to meet her direct supervisor at the new job and discuss what does. That company is also still a client to this day.

Later, the organization that I had interviewed with for its and benefits manager role, and in which I had shared a depth of information with the interviewer, also became a client. When I met with the CEO of the organization, he was really impressed with my depth of knowledge and ability to guide them with their international hires. I don't think he ever knew that his organization actually had an opportunity to have me internal but didn't act on it.

Educating People

As I did more and more research on the types of businesses in the Huntsville area, I found that my assumption about it having no international business was completely wrong. It had many companies that conducted business all around the world. That made me wonder whether they were being compliant and managing the human capital pieces correctly—or even cared.

But a big obstacle I faced was that companies in the Huntsville area didn't know what I did or why they should care. I decided that I needed to educate people. I began to offer myself as a subject matter expert and deliver training classes to groups in human resources, international trade, and government. I joined associations and looked for other places to be where I might interact with companies or organizations that needed my services.

Then I started to host large conferences. After all, I had been going to those types of events for more than twenty years; maybe I could organize some and get people interested in attending. I contacted a few former colleagues and suppliers and convinced them to be guest speakers at the events I hosted.

Since no one really knew me, I with a large volunteer organization to publicize the event under their banner. This was a new area of business for them, and so they were happy to explore the idea with me.

My first conference, which took place about one year after I started , was on : "Doing Business Globally—What You Don't Know Could Hurt You." I brought in speakers from firms such as Global, , Insights Discovery*, , and Coca-Cola. More than one hundred people attended, and it was the start of people in the area truly understanding the service I offered and why they needed it.

Business Jesus Has Our Backs

Time and again, I began to see how when I wasn't afraid to put myself out there and didn't try to control every aspect of the business but instead trusted that my Business Jesus had my back, amazing things would happen. Let me tell you about Business Jesus.

I believe that if you have Jesus in your heart and as part of your DNA, you can't separate him out. It's part of that "authentic you" that people talk about so often. Well, for me, as a Christian, that authentic you is being a Christian in business, so that's where I find my Business Jesus. There can be a Doctor Jesus, Stylist Jesus, Rock Star Jesus, Professor Jesus, Teacher Jesus; for me, it's Business Jesus. He comes with me when I go into meetings, when I'm up on a stage, when I need to counsel an employee, or when I need to make a difficult and often an overwhelming decision. I trust his counsel, and it helps me better understand when I feel calm about a decision and when I feel chaotic about one. I know that his voice talking to me gives me conviction and strength to do what I need to do.

Growing Pains

Even as I began to get clients onboard, the business was getting by—just barely—on my severance package from the Asia-based company. The package got me through one year, and it allowed me to set up, design, and start some basic networking and advertising. But when the second year came around, I needed a line of credit. The only significant income we had was Mark's paychecks—I wasn't even taking a salary from the business.

When I told Mark about this, he looked at me for a long time and said, "Are you sure about this? Our family is in a good financial place now, our home is paid off, and we have plenty of income. I don't want you to jeopardize our personal life for this 'hobby' that you insist on pursuing."

"This is what I want to do," I said firmly, "and more importantly, I know that it's what God wants me to do."

Mark could see how much it meant to me, and he said I would have his support. That's one of the reasons our marriage has always been strong—when push comes to shove, we're always on each other's side, no matter what.

I still remember the moment at the bank when we signed the paperwork for the $250,000 line of credit. I felt a mixture of happiness, pride, and anxiety, all at the same time. At that point, it was put up or shut up—I knew I had to make this thing work. To this day, the company is self-funded; we have not taken on any investors, so we are also not beholden to anyone to change our direction or focus on growing money rather than growing people. I know that by following

Jesus's direction, the money and the business will keep coming. He brings me opportunities every day, and it is up to me to do the most with the gift of entrepreneurship that I can, to be a good steward for his business, and to take care of his people. That is my job, and if I can do it well, everyone benefits.

Starting to Grow and Hire

One of the hardest things about the human capital solutions business is being able to determine the difference between strategic consulting and task administration. The first two years of the business were mostly consulting work, where I would go in and redesign organizations internally. But companies would just use our services for a couple of years, learn all of our tips and tricks, and then decide they didn't need us anymore. Those early years we didn't have long-term assignments; I just reorganized other companies' processes. We've since then reorganized and become a full-fledged outsourcing firm.

In the early years, as the company began to grow, I slowly brought in some part-time interns and then eventually began to grow full-time employees. At first, my staff couldn't do the high-level strategic consulting I was doing, so I needed to delegate task administration to them, which meant there were questions to be answered: What was I to delegate? How would I train the team? What would I charge for the service?

I was working with a volunteer organization in my city, Women's Business Center of North Alabama (). They had volunteer coaches who were executives who had started their own businesses, sold them, and then started other ones. The cost was either free or very low to me, as a new entrepreneur.

As part of the coaching, one of the first things I had to do was sit down and think about every single task that was required to do every bit of the administration of the client-facing business. Then I had to think about how long should it take to do these tasks, what level should be doing them, the costs of doing the task, and finally what I could charge clients to do these tasks. That was how I could start to think about whether or not I could make any profit from this side of the business while also teaching my new staff a skill they didn't have before.

Knock Three Times

I continued to ask for God's guidance and knew I had to learn how to be willing to seize the opportunities as he presented them to me. As James 4:2 (KJV) says, "Ye have not, because ye ask not." But it took three attempts before I recognized one of the biggest opportunities to come our way.

Business had started coming in from all kinds of sources. I would get an email or phone call from a large prospect that wanted to work with them. That always amazed me because it usually would be a proposal request that we had not even known about.

One such opportunity came knocking three times before I even realized it was legitimate. After receiving some information at a luncheon networking event about getting a government schedule and certification to be a Women-Owned Small Business (), I thought, "Yes, we should do this." It took a year of time, effort, and funding to put everything in place, and over the twelve months that I navigated all the rules and paperwork, I wasn't even sure exactly *how* to do business with the US government. Most of my international experience had been in the corporate world with the commercial manufacturing industry, and any colleagues who had worked in the government fields had worked only as government contractors.

One day, after we were scheduled and certified, I received an email from an organization requesting additional information on the foreign payroll bid we had recently submitted—since I hadn't submitted such a bid, I ignored the email thinking it was spam. Then I received an email through my website, asking the same thing. Again, I hadn't submitted anything, so I just ignored it. Finally, I received a phone call directly from the agency that had sent the email. When I finally did speak with someone, they informed me that, due to my certification within the government system, they had identified me and wanted to talk with me about the payroll services I could provide.

Wow, I was blown away! That's how we began doing foreign employment services with the US government and ultimately became the Foreign Global Employer of Record in more than forty countries, but we landed on it after simply letting Business Jesus have our backs. When it came to the government contract work, I was tasked to do the ground work, utilize my skills, network, and get to know people, and then he would do the rest. That first contract became word of mouth to other agencies, and today, that is a $10 million per year business for , and it continues to grow.

Keeping the Culture

We made our first million dollars three years after the company started. So, we had some revenue, but I was investing every bit of it back into the company, with new personnel, new lines of business, and new companies. But what an exhilarating time that was! I truly felt that we were on our way, but I knew I had a lot more work to do before we'd become profitable.

We had the foundation in place and were moving forward, but I started to feel uneasy about handling things when we gained more momentum, grew faster, and brought in more team members. How could I keep the culture of the company—the caring internal environment I had created—intact amid such a fast-changing environment?

I knew I couldn't achieve it through my authority alone. I had an idea of a different kind of authority held by many people across the organization. It would be based on Christian standards, and I thought it had great potential, but would it work? Admittedly, there were challenges.

For instance, one of the first full-time people whom I hired was a very intelligent young woman who was pretty vocal about her atheism, and she supervised a young woman who was very vocal about her faith. It was a nonbeliever/believer situation that wasn't the best fit from the start. At one point, the two had a confrontation, which started when the believer signed her email salutation with "Blessings." It was unusual, but it didn't really bother me. In fact, I was impressed with her ability to put herself out there. However, her direct supervisor, the nonbeliever, said it made her feel uncomfortable and that it was perceived as a judgment on others; that had to be a terrible feeling for her. I brought both of them together to have a conversation, and the employee stated that she had always signed her emails that way, but she had not worked in a corporate environment before. She agreed to be less out there.

This was one time that I probably should have left it alone and allowed Jesus to do his work between them instead of me doing it, but that incident made me realize that discrimination about faith can go both ways: both nonbelievers and believers may feel they're being judged.

It's taken a while to figure out, and there was turnover at first. As I've said, it's not required to be a Christian to work at the company, but once all of the people who decided that a Christian culture wasn't a good fit for them moved on, amazing things began happening—better morale, more connectivity, just clearly God giving his people the things they need to succeed. Staff meetings often begin with prayer to remind everyone of the blessings that the company has been privileged to experience and to ensure that everything is done in a way that is helping people.

A Big Responsibility

As the company continued to grow, we ultimately had to start breaking it down into smaller companies. I didn't really understand just how big the company was getting, though, until one employee told me she had just moved out of her parents' house and was renting her first apartment. That's when it really hit me—I'm responsible for these people! If didn't fly, they wouldn't be able to pay rent.

Once I realized that, I thought, "You've got a responsibility to these people; what are you going to do with it?" I admit, there are days when I want to quit, but I think God gave me the responsibility to make the foundation of this company.

Today, there are seven interconnected companies in Group. Each started as part of that center of excellence concept that I had developed while working in corporate organizations. As each one came to have more clients and expand into other states and other countries, I knew we needed to separate them out from other parts of the business. There are special talents that are required for each of these, and it made sense to set them up this way. It allows each of those companies to continue to grow in their specialty while bringing in other parts of the group to augment their capabilities.

The companies are Talent Mobility Solutions, a relocation management company (), which is full outsourcing of relocation management; ˙ International Solutions, which is our payroll solutions company; Clark Global Institute, a training company; Business Systems Solutions, through which the tool Employee Global Logistics (˙) is licensed to companies; International Benefits Brokerage, which offers benefits solutions; International Consulting, our first consulting and program management company; and Holding Group, our corporate conglomerate.

While we have much more structure in place today, I still have no final idea where we're ultimately going, but wherever it is, it's going to be good. I may take more risk than a lot of people would, but then, anyone who starts a company is taking a very big risk. But I know if we're good at what we do and put people first, then God is going to steer us in the right direction. As I say all the time, "Why not us?"

Points to Ponder

1. What are some ways that your company can improve the connections between colleagues?

2. Are there work interactions that you can change from virtual to face-to-face?

3. Think about how you send the message to customers and partners that you're a faith-based company—are there ways that you can do that more effectively?

4. Can you create confidential situations at work where employees are comfortable talking to you about nearly anything they need help with?

5. Are there ways in which you can include prayer and/or Bible study in employees' weekly work schedules?

Chapter 5

The Value of Humanization in Globalization

May the God who gives endurance and encouragement give you the same attitude of mind toward each other that Christ Jesus had, so that with one mind and one voice you may glorify the God and Father of our Lord Jesus Christ.

——————————————— —ROMANS 15:5-7 ———————

When the world went to a virtual workplace, it began to desensitize humanity. After two years of being apart, not being face-to-face, not getting on airplanes to fly to a conference, people are feeling more alone today than ever before. Sure, they can see you on video, but they can't shake your hand, touch you, give you a hug—none of that human touch that is so important. It's different when you can sit in a room and maybe have a meal with you or a glass of wine, to actually touch someone or see their body language. There's just a pulse when you're in the same room that you don't get on a . Yes, it's more time-consuming and costly to get on a plane or drive to see someone, but even if they're only an hour away, going to their place of business, sitting down with them, and having that connection make all the difference. That's all part of our humanization.

Humans Are Not Meant to Be Alone

In Genesis, God created Eve so that Adam would not be alone: "The Lord God said, 'It is not good for the man to be alone. I will make a helper suitable for him.'" We were never meant to be alone; we need one another. We need that connection.

When you lose that connection, you lose some of the ability to form a relationship. And often that's with people we're spending more than forty hours each week with. If you're spending that much time together, you want to have a relationship with those people.

Before the COVID-19 pandemic changed the way we interact and work, people used to say, "Business happens in the hallways," meaning that colleagues had meaningful, up-close-and-personal discussions outside the office setting. (I can safely say that happens in the ladies' room as well.) Before we all went remote, we were at work at six o'clock in the morning, and by four o'clock in the afternoon, it was time for a drink because we were all so exhausted. But without any real connection, it was just work; there wasn't a relationship.

With virtual, we've lost the small things that mean so much—the hand gestures (no, emojis won't replace them), tone of voice, and facial expressions that help us connect with more than just words. Since we work with a lot of government agencies, many of which don't have camera usage on their work computers, true connection doesn't really happen virtually.

Our former vice president of operations, Scott Murray, has a unique perspective on working virtually:

> I was a police officer for thirty years, and even in the midst of COVID, the police don't have the option of working from home—they still have to be on the streets and up close with people whom they're trying to apprehend or

trying to help.... At , we support remote work, but I know from my experience there's nothing like being face-to-face with someone—you can combine their words with their facial expressions and body language and get a lot more information than you can in a call that is done virtually. Those cues help you take a conversation in a different, and often very productive, direction that can make a big difference in the outcome.

Together, We Communicate Better

Humans communicate with more than just words. Individuals communicate based on their culture and how they were raised, so what I write and how you read what I wrote are never the same things. For instance, I am a very blunt and to-the-point type of person. If the person I am communicating with reads what I write, it may come off as offensive. I also express very few emotions in anything I write or speak, but if someone is reading what I write with a lot of emotions, they will read things into the verbiage that was never intended.

Once when I was out of the office on travel for two weeks, one of our managers, I'll call him Sam, texted me a question. I texted him back with my normal, yes, no, maybe type of response, written with absolutely no emotion whatsoever. A few days went by, and Sam reached out to me (via text) to ask if I was upset with him. That question really floored me because I immediately thought, "Why? Is there something I should be upset about?"

I reread the conversation from a few days before and realized that I had perceived what he wrote as asking a question, to which I simply answered yes. But to Sam, my one-word sentence meant that I really wasn't OK with something he had done—maybe I wanted something different. What Sam was looking for was some affirmation beyond just a one-word response. If I had texted, "Sam, that's a great idea, and I'm glad you are moving that process forward, thank you," or if the same conversation had happened in the office, his next few days would not have been filled with emotions.

Even though, as I said, I'm a very to-the-point kind of person, I sometimes find myself in a similar situation as Sam. Just as I was working on this portion of the book, an email came in from a German colleague. The email was matter-of-fact on what she could and could not do. Now, as a culture, Germans are known for being very matter-of-fact, so it shouldn't have surprised me that there was no emotion in the email, just the facts about the task. However, when I read it, I initially thought that she was pushing back on me, second-guessing my instructions and just being difficult. How easily the matter could have escalated being just email correspondence with no human interconnection.

Connecting Globally

Globalization is about getting your products out there and expanding your business reach. But products don't sell themselves; people do that. If you want to work globally, you have to be able to connect with people globally. And while people are people around the globe, globalization means working with different cultures. That doesn't mean understanding culture alone, because then you're still talking about traits. You have to go deeper than that: you have to understand the person, the personal behaviors—these are humans, with lives, spouses, kids, churches, and so on. Actively listening with your eyes and ears will only go so far; you must also listen with your heart in order to touch someone in a moment when they might need it most.

That goes beyond learning whether to bow or shake hands; it's about understanding and connecting with people. It's about understanding different behaviors and energies. As a leader, it's about looking at the people first: How do we take care of the people and include everyone in the mission and then actually accomplish that mission? At a time of great change, when people are probably more open to other ways of seeing the world than they have ever been, how do we reimagine the future of work? How do we put humanization back in the workplace?

For instance, Asian culture may be known as very driven and detail-oriented, but that's not necessarily about the people. When I was working in Asia, two males who wanted to work for the team were told that if they worked for a woman, their career was over. That was difficult to hear and digest, even though the manager who said it respected me and thought highly of me, and I knew that Asian culture and American culture were not the same. I had to put aside my personal desire to prove myself to the top executive and realize this was about the manager, his needs, and the ability to move ahead in a culture and an organization that I was less likely to be a part of for the long term.

In Asian cultures, the school you attend, the job you have, and the family you marry into are extremely important and affect not only you but also your family and your family to be. It's a kind of culture Americans cannot even imagine; the United States is an "employment at-will state," meaning an employee can leave a position or be fired. How would an American college graduate feel if a job interview included his parents to help them understand and agree to the opportunity the company was giving their son or daughter and to ensure that everyone was devoted and connected to the company and its values and that the new employee would be dedicated and give their full attention to the company? How many young females in the United States would be willing to leave their new baby with their parents for two years, only seeing the child on weekends, just to ensure that they could give all of their time and attention to their new job?

In that culture, a person can't leave their job without inflicting shame on the entire family. It was an incredible amount of pressure to know that I was responsible not only for an employee's career progression but also for the success of the employee's family, parents, and future offspring.

Yet even in that culture, people's individual personalities needed to be nurtured. For instance, one Asian female on the team was not about details, but she was about vision; how could her vision bring value to a detail-oriented team and help accomplish the mission? In a culture that values detail and analytics, that expects the employee to listen quietly and do as they are instructed, and that values age above experience or vision, what place is there for someone with a question-ing nature, an outspoken and focused young female who only needs a bit of coaching and encouraging? How could I help nurture her ability to see beyond doing as you are told to seeing the possibilities of the organization, and where it might go? (Ultimately, there was simply no place for such a person in that role, so she moved on and is now a global HR manager at a major corporation.)

So, humanization in globalization is about understanding others. It's about respecting the culture, whatever that may be, wherever you are, and overcoming stereotypes. For instance, it's often thought that pretty, blond, American women can't have brains too, which is abso-lutely not true, or that people in Italy don't work hard and are lazy because they take naps—they work just as hard, they just work much later in the day, and they have good work-life balance. American culture is all about everyone being equal and engaged. Right now, there's a big push for diversity, equity, and inclusion (DEI). But it's not enough just to have people at the table; those voices all need to be heard. Unfortunately, if everyone has a voice, no one can be heard, and nothing moves forward. It's not that way in the rest of the world.

But we can let voices be heard and still move forward if we understand the behaviors that motivate people.

Personality versus Behavior

At , it's about understanding behavioral preferences, understanding the behaviors that drive a person. That's different from personality. Personality is something people are born with; it's not something they *learn*. Behavior, however, is learned.

That needs to be understood when dealing with assessments that look at different personalities. Those are great for understanding *personality*. But behaviors are what's really important when talking about DEI.

was the DEI champion in the small business category for Huntsville in 2022, an award granted not only because we have a lot of different nationalities working for us but also because we get below the skin level. There's no denying a person's skin color, but we look beyond that. We want to understand the behaviors that drive a person. How do they treat other people? What motivates them, and what them? When they sit down at the table, what baggage do they bring, and how do we unpack that to get the best out of them? How do they cooperate with other teams, and how do we help that team form?

That's why we've been so successful with our workforce development. We motivate people based on their behaviors, because people can change their behaviors, but they can't change their personality.

That's what the humanization of globalization is about; it's about understanding the behaviors that drive people on a global basis rather than stereotyping different nationalities, genders, age groups, or other elements. Jesus didn't recognize or judge people based on religious or personal or ethnic backgrounds. Soldiers, fisherman, tax collectors, prostitutes—he loved them all the same. Why do we think we are above this? When we put faith, color, and socioeconomic background as a major point, are we not the same as a Pharisee?

When you work globally, you have to get down below the skin level to the behaviors of the person to really make teams work, especially when working with remote areas and remote .

A lot of books have been written about cultural and language training. Those are very important things to know because different cultures have different values. In the Middle East, you don't shake hands with your left hand; in Asia, when first greeting someone, you place your hands by your side and bow, and then if you're handing them a business card, you do it with both hands.

Those are cultural norms. They are very much a part of a first impression, but they don't have anything to do with the person. Once you get past those cultural norms and get to know who the person is, you can understand what drives them. Earlier, I talked about how the Asia-based company wanted me to drink and learn karaoke; the reason for that was so they could get to know the real me.

Understanding the Difference

Here's an example of what it means to understand behavior versus personality.

We've all been in the room with a contrarian, that person who, no matter what you say, is going to take the opposite side. For instance, let's say someone in the group is such a terrible team player that everyone agrees the person needs to be fired—except for that one person who is compelled to defend the poor performer, citing unfairness or that they haven't been given enough chances. That's different from a nurturing behavior, someone who is always trying to make sure that everyone is taken care of, who is always trying to build morale and really cares about people themselves.

A nurturing *behavior preference* is typically calm, quiet, and listening, but this behavioral preference can have bad days too. What does that look like? On a bad day, they basically shut down and can even become stubborn or unmovable—very unusual behavior for them. For instance, in the example of getting rid of the poor performer, even a nurturing personality will often agree at some point that enough is enough. But if that same should suddenly change their mind and begin defending the poor performer, is it because they are actually not a but instead a passive/aggressive *personality* or because they're simply having a bad day, which is a *behavioral* issue?

Dealing with people often means looking at your own behavior. For instance, you can't change a passive/aggressive personality, but you can change how you behave toward that personality. If you know you've got a contrarian on your team, then you can start by speaking their speak, but then let them talk.

"I know you're concerned about this person's welfare and whether we've given them enough changes," you might say. Then ask, "What do you think we could do to maybe champion them and turn them around?"

"Well," they might say, "we could do this and that."

"Those are great ideas. Have we done those things?" you reply.

"Well, yes, we have."

"OK, well, what else could we do?"

"We could do this, this, and this."

"Those are great ideas too. Can you see about implementing them?"

Before you know it, they will have talked themselves out of their position because you allowed them to speak.

That's humanization in the workplace, and it's a really big part of the workforce development that we do for organizations. Clients often tell us our training is revolutionary, but it's really about understanding *what* to care about and getting below the surface into who people are.

Taking the Time to Learn

It's actually very difficult for senior management to grasp the concept of humanization, but it's because there is very little training about this for middle managers. That's what we address with our supervisor-employee relationship training, which then helps executive leaders know how to be executive managers by the time they get there.

Beyond training, however, what's needed is to take time to learn more about the person. Everybody has time for that; it only takes a few seconds. I've had to retrain myself in picking up on different behaviors of people very quickly, even people whom I know very well.

Now I can tell when someone is stressed or has a problem. When someone comes to my office, stands in the doorway, and says, "Hey, Debbie, I've got a question," then they really need me to just stop what I'm doing for about five seconds, nod my head as I'm listening to them, and then give them a yes, no, maybe. But if they come in and pull up a chair and sit down in front of my desk, I know they need to talk to me. They need my attention. They need me to stop what I'm doing and just let them talk.

Anyone has the ability to pick up all those behaviors because we've all done them ourselves. The same is true with personalities. You know how you naturally react to certain situations, so it can be a real challenge to learn how to pick up on different behaviors and find those behaviors in yourself in order to better understand that behavior in someone else.

In one of my leadership roles, I remember very distinctly how a young subordinate "seemed" to question everything I did. I began to take personal offense to this and "read" so much more into this action than was really there. Only when I really looked at myself and began to know more about my personal behaviors did I realize that I was really a terrible communicator. While I run a million miles a minute and have so much in my head, I forget that others do not do this. Their behavior may be to slow down, critically look at each task, and how best to do it, and often, they may not even want to start the task until they are fully versed on what the task is, why the task is important, and what the final outcome is expected to be. When I slowed down and gave this subordinate the information he needed in a timely manner, and with enough time to complete the task, he was able to then complete it.

Too often, we mistake lack of communication because of a cultural view: "Asians need consensus before they can agree to move forward, Germans need full details on tasks, Americans are work-aholics." Now throw into the mix the language issues and remote work or only written communication, and wow, what a mess we can easily have.

When we slow down and treat others as described in Luke 5:5–11, how Jesus uses everyday work and common tasks to bring us together to help and connect with our fellow human beings in whatever capacity we may be in, during that particular moment, we can start to see the value of connecting and treat one another with love and respect.

Points to Ponder

1. How are you looking at your peers, your subordinates, and your superiors? Are you trying to bring out the best in them or more worried about them not seeing you? Are you using your skills in behavioral preferences to make a situation, a person, or an organization better each day?

2. Are you taking a chance and stepping outside of your comfort zone so that you have the opportunity and preparation to say yes when you are confronted? What efforts have you made today to better understand where someone else is coming from?

3. How do you get your information? Do you wait for others to give it to you, or are you going out and finding it for yourself? Are you expanding your mind and skill set by reading new and different things, trying a different approach, and having an open mind about a different way of doing things?

Chapter 6

Informal Leadership

Go, gather together all the Jews who are in Susa, and fast for me. Do not eat or drink for three days, night or day. I and my attendants will fast as you do. When this is done, I will go to the king, even though it is against the law. And if I perish, I perish.

—ESTHER 4:16

The story of Esther in the Bible gives a wonderful example of informal leadership. An orphan, the beautiful Esther found favor with powerful King of Persia. Though she was crowned Queen of Persia, she had no authority to rule, other than over her servants. She didn't set policy or change the direction of the kingdom, but she had great influence among the women in the king's harem and the people of Persia.

Esther was the adopted daughter of Mordecai, who was a Jew. Mordecai's bitter enemy in the court of the king was , the king's right-hand man. Because Mordecai failed to bow before , devised a scheme to have him and every Jew in Persia killed. Mordecai called on Queen Esther to save her people.

Esther had the courage to risk the king's wrath by appearing before him without invitation, which was in violation of the law. She made up her mind that if she died for approaching the king, so be it.

Esther persuaded the king to save her people and hang on the very gallows he built for Mordecai. The king revised his edict to kill the Jews, and the Jews got their revenge on their would-be persecutors and celebrated—this was the beginning of the festival of Purim.

Esther showed the qualities of a great informal leader. Although she had no authority, she had built strong relationships with the people of the kingdom, they believed in her, and she cared about them. She had the courage to take the lead and rally them to fight for their lives—risking her life in the process.

Informal Leadership = Influence

Formal and informal leaders get their authority from different sources. Formal leaders' authority comes from the hierarchy of the organization in which they operate. Someone in a leadership position has the power to make decisions and delegate tasks because their title gives them that authority.

On the contrary, informal leaders have no authority, but they do have influence. Informal leaders understand people and how to work with their traits and give them what they need. They know how to connect to understand who the person is and "speak their language" in a way that makes sense to them. Their power is based on the trust that people place in them, shared interests, relationships with their colleagues, and the good reputation they've earned in the workplace. Their coworkers recognize the qualities, not the title, of an informal leader.[2] They may not have managerial tasks in their daily work, but they still do things to make an organization run smoothly and create a productive, cordial work environment.

---

2   Indeed Editorial Team, "Formal vs. Informal Leadership: Definitions and Differences," Indeed, last modified March 10, 2023, https://www.indeed.com/career-advice/career-development/formal-and-informal-leadership.

The informal leader knows how to inspire people and motivate by adapting to what works for the individual. For instance, I can't figure out spreadsheets, but one of the people in our accounting group loves them—she will gladly take them off my hands and run with them. I love seeing that. On the contrary, we have an employee who will wither and die if she's forced to stay in a cubicle all day; a social butterfly will not excel if placed in a black box. But task her with getting out and telling the PZI story, and there's no stopping her. Give people what they love to do, and they'll do it without question.

It's not always obvious what it takes to motivate people. I'm a CPA and an international tax accountant. I know tax code in countries around the world; don't take me down the tax road because it's hard for me to get back to the human piece. Naturally, you might think I would be someone very detail-oriented, very structured, very analytical—but that's just not me. My behavior is more driven by the mission and a deadline, and we'll use the tax code to accomplish that. So, while I'll use analytics to get the job done, that's not my go-to behavioral preference.

Traits of a Great Informal Leader

One reason informal leaders can influence other employees positively is because they have credibility in their organization. Colleagues think it's a good move to follow them.

Informal leaders tend to be people of action. They consistently jump to it and say, "Hey, why don't you and I get together and do this?" I see that happen at PZI all the time. At PZI, we value innovation and believe that the best ideas don't always come from the formal leaders. There is nothing I love more than to have a new informal leader take a "tried-and-true methodology" and come up with a better, smarter, more efficient way of doing it. I tell my employees all the time, "Hey, I'm a baby boomer; if there is a hard, ugly, manual way to do something, I will find it. Please make it better." We believe in collaboration because we know that, with a team effort, we can bring possible alternatives to the "process" in order to make it more efficient and give it a better flow to the outcome and to ensure that our "product"—to service others— comes through loud and clear. Our best informal leaders are the ones who will approach their group leaders and let them know what the feeling of the group may be, including whether something needs to be clarified or explained more in depth.

Informal leaders make a human connection—with the heart, not just with the head. How many times have you heard someone say, "I don't agree with his decision, but he's the boss, so we just have to go with it?" Often, a team won't give an all-out effort because there's no connection—the boss doesn't really care about his people. With good informal leadership, power comes from caring. Our informal leaders are the ones "rallying the troops" and also the ones letting the formal leadership know when a direction could be better served by going a slightly different direction. They are great at managing up, down, and horizontal. There are many ways to get to a target, and sometimes going straight ahead only blows up the target without accomplishing the effect of bringing the group along for the win and the victory. At PZI, informal leaders don't just make a connection with the group, but they also work and collaborate with others and build connections with their peers and their superiors. That connection of trust that an informal leader has is the influence they are able to bring with them on the way to the victory. They ensure the group cohesion remains together, and they look for the outliers on the fringes that may need to be brought into the group or that the group needs to steer clear of.

One of my favorite informal leaders loves to welcome new employees in; I don't mean with handshakes but with confetti on their desks, welcome signs, and often even with balloons. What an amazing first day the new person has when they know they are wanted and people are happy they are there. I don't remember that ever happening in any job when I started. That's why I love the people that I am so very fortunate to call the PZI family. It truly is a family, and I'm lucky to have been a part of starting it.

Great informal leaders are generous with their time and efforts. They know the things that an organization needs, and they work tirelessly toward those goals, even though they don't receive any tangible benefit from doing so. Our informal leaders show up in so many ways, especially with their generous time and efforts. It might be the remembrance of birthdays, the checking on the colleague that didn't come in because they were feeling under the weather, or chipping in on a project that they have nothing to do with just to help take down the stress level of other colleagues.

It is not uncommon for (we'll call her Cathy) to be burning the midnight oil or even to be one of the last ones leaving the office. She always checks on everyone else and makes sure that if she isn't the last one out, that anyone left is aware of their surroundings and who is still in the office. Having that little bit of caring and conscientiousness sets her apart. She often even checks on me, if I happen to still be at my desk when she leaves, just to make sure I'm good to go and don't need anything else from her.

Informal leaders know their organization well. That sound knowledge of the company's history, leadership, culture, and policies lets them focus their leadership efforts on the company's mission by sharing important policies. Informal leaders don't just know their organization, but they believe in their organizational missions and goals, as well. They ensure by their efforts that the goals and missions they live by conform to the organization's. If not, they know it is not the organization for them, and they are not afraid to step out to find the right group, the right project, or even the right organization. That's what's so powerful about an informal leader; they hold true to themselves. That sense of self and caring comes through loud and clear, and informal leaders who care about the organization and want to see it grow and succeed are always the best leaders. They mentor and groom other informal leaders to take their place, and then those people often move on into formal leadership roles themselves.

My favorite cheerleader in the organization is the formal leader who has worked her way up from an hourly informal employee to one of my exec staff. She loves to tell the story (and it is true) that I turned her down for a job for over a year. She believes in our mission and knows that we are people of faith committed to doing right for people and making changes in people's lives. Nothing more complicated than that. To watch her grow from a person who offered to volunteer for me to being one of my execs is really impressive. People love to work for her and with her. She ensures that she does this every day, and if I ever forget that is our mission, she is there cheering me on and reminding me who we work for—and it isn't the shareholders. We answer to one authority, our Business Jesus, who guides us in battle and blesses us in rewards.

Effective informal leaders are great at establishing and nurturing relationships across the organization. They don't just interact with a small group of people; they get to know many people at all levels. Making friends and building good communication help them establish trust and loyalty, which are valuable when leading others. An informal leader will look around at the group they work and collaborate with and will work with and mentor the group they have, instead of trying to transition to "another group." In corporate roles, so often, I've seen leaders and staff state, "If that person wasn't in our group, it would be so much better." Well, that person is in the group, and it is the influence of the informal leader that brings out the best in every person in a group and helps to mold them for the betterment of the formal leadership. Often knowing someone in a group has your back and listens to you, even if you don't think your boss or your leader listens or understands you, is what makes the difference in a person staying with an organization, turning around an attitude, or deciding that the organization is not the right fit for them.

As a formal leader, I try to ensure that we don't get rid of people too quickly. I really struggle with letting anyone go. Hence, why they don't let me do the hiring anymore. While the motto today is hire slow and fire fast, we must really look at the individual and determine whether we have done our best for that individual or if they are simply in the wrong place. So many of my informal leaders have taken the reins on this and adopted someone into their department who was in another department and failing miserably, but rather than firing that person, the informal leader encouraged them to give another situation within PZI a try. It doesn't always work, unfortunately, but when it does, the feeling of accomplishment that we made in that person's self-worth is triple paid back to us over the course of our company mission.

Informal leaders tend to be great listeners. They want to know the opinions and suggestions of many of their coworkers before they make important decisions. They care about everyone whom the decision affects, not just which decision is best for their own interests.[3] Informal leaders understand and buy into the mission of the organization, and

3   Valencia Higuera, "How to Make Employees Feel Like You Value Their Opinion," CareerAddict, July 12, 2014, https://www.careeraddict.com/make-employees-feel-like-you-value-their-opinion.

they support decisions that foster that mission. By utilizing their own active listening skills and natural mentoring techniques, they are truly able to understand and often explain the organization's why behind a decision. Their intuition and caring of others help them to use empathy with their groups and colleagues, and often that one thing is enough to bring someone back into the group mix rather than on the outskirts or in opposition.

I really love how this informal leader calmly and quickly talks to everyone. Their kind nature shows through in everything they do. Even when they are stressed or upset, they are naturally calm and quietly explain any concerns. Then they step back and listen to what others have to say, sometimes agreeing and sometimes not but always listening and taking others' opinions into consideration.

Also, informal leaders have a capability that many formal leaders don't, simply because they don't hold a position of designated authority—they can say things to team members that are off-limits for someone in an official management role who must have a more formal, "corporate" approach.

The PZI Approach

In our organization, informal leaders are aligned with the Christian values of caring for people and supporting people—being the hands and feet of Jesus. I tell people who are applying for a position at PZI that they don't have to be a Christian to work for us, but they have to have the Christian values of caring for others, treating people with dignity, and working together as a team. We are more than "customer service"; we want to ensure both our employees and our clients are getting the PZI treatment in everything we do.

Our strategy and proposal manager at PZI, Heather Conkle, explains how informal leadership works at the company:

It's an integral part of working at PZI. We tend to be very supportive of one another and collaborate with our coworkers outside of our departments. Job titles might define our pay scale, but they don't define our roles. Part of that is because PZI employees are very utilitarian: as a small company, many of us work in multiple departments—this allows us to bond quickly and encourage one another.

Informal leadership at our company looks a lot like peer-to-peer mentorship: taking a few moments throughout the day to invest in relationships with coworkers, having casual conversations about problem-solving, and offering support.

People in our company who are mid-level coordinators pull people off to the side and have direct, meaningful conversations, in which they try to lead the person to a better situation or frame of mind. That informal leadership happens because of the solid relationships they have cultivated.

Seven times each year, PZI conducts a weeklong course on informal leadership at Army University. Everything we teach in the course is seen through the lens of relationships: influence, impact, situational leadership, handling difficult conversations, building connections, leading through turbulence, and searching for work-life balance.

Several people on our team are licensed practitioners of the behavioral assessment tool Insights Discovery®, which focuses on personal accountability for behaviors. The core of the program is the importance of relationships for enhancing the team—and subsequently, our business—as a whole.

Real Talk (a.k.a. Active Listening)

Active listening is a must-have skill set for leaders today, formal or informal leaders. What is active listening? Active listening helps to understand someone's preferences, whether through the way they speak, their word choices, or their body language. It's also about listening to your team or actively listening to God and letting him talk to you.

Yet, it's more than being attentive or engaged in the moment with the participant; it's more a learned skill of repeating what you heard, to ensure it is what the person said or what they meant. It allows the participant who is speaking to clarify any misunderstanding immediately with the listener rather than later hearing something that was not at all what you thought you had said. I can't tell you how many times our teams have used this skill on one another and even on me.

Active listening is one of the tools that we teach in our workshops. We teach not just how to hear the words but also how to take the time to listen to the words, discover how those words were given, the body language used, and the behaviors behind them.

One of the best ways to make sure everyone is engaged is to communicate as much as humanly possible. For leaders, that means a lot more than just, "Hello, how are you?" It's fine to have a quick chat, but you need to prioritize "real talk," which is more than cheering on your team and telling them how great they're doing. Instead, it's being open and honest, and it won't be all compliments. Tell your people where they're performing at a high level, as well as let them know how they can improve. Make sure they know where there's room for growth.

Then and Now as a Leader

When I was a young manager at a large accounting firm, I remember being told by a male supervisor, "You need to be as aggressive as hell and don't take no for an answer." In the military lifestyle, you must make a decision; you cannot *not* make a decision. Mark has always said, even a bad decision is better than no decision at all. So that's the leader I was: aggressive and get it done. I was driving the bus, but I was on the bus alone more times than not. I had left my team back at the bus stop and plowed straight through the tunnel without them. What that meant was *no one had my back*.

In my corporate career, I was a very controlled leader. I felt like I was getting beat up pretty much all the time from my leadership, so I could never let go of any control. But there was something else. In my corporate life, I thought that I was protecting my staff, keeping them from getting run over. So, I would take the blame for mistakes, or I would do other things to protect them but never let them know what the results of those mistakes would be. But what I didn't realize was that I shut them out, and that was a lack of transparency, in their eyes. They saw me as taking credit for their work. It didn't really cross my mind that I wasn't allowing them to grow, that I wasn't allowing them to make the mistakes, and that they would actually learn from those mistakes. That type of transformation in anyone is where real growth happens. That's how I learned—I made mistakes. As leaders, we are not parents to our employees; we're their colleagues, their mentors. We're not supposed to try to shield them, yet, at the same time, we don't want to overwhelm them. But it's not for you to decide what's going to help them or hurt them; it's up to them.

When I worked for other organizations, I kept taking all the stress, all the burden, on my own shoulders. And I held it so tight that it just made me miserable and made those around me miserable. I've got more than forty employees now, and it's a lot of pressure, but I know that it's going to grow and be whatever God wants it to be. I have to pray that he gives me the wisdom to make the right choices, say the right words, focus where he needs me to focus, and do what I need to do. Utilizing a leadership attitude of togetherness, sharing of responsibility as well as successes or failures, most definitely has made a transformation in my leadership from being *the* leader to empowering many informal leaders to take the reins and grow with the responsibility.

Today, I know that people learn from their mistakes. While no one likes failure, and I've had my share of those, every one of them has taught me such a valuable lesson and made me into the leader I am today: one who expects her team to make mistakes, to grow from those mistakes, and to experience those same feelings that made me realize I didn't want to fail again. But it's how we react to others and the grace we show to one another during those times that really show what a leader is. Jesus shows us all grace, even when we don't deserve it—thank God he does! The transformational attitude that can come from making mistakes and learning from them, especially when used by both formal and informal leadership, can make the difference in not only the type of leader you become but also the type of organization you impact.

The good leader has the confidence in themselves to know they don't have to be possessive of decision-making. Most of my corporate career, someone was breathing down my neck to get it done, do this, do that. I'm a type A personality anyway, so getting it done is in my DNA. But I've had to learn through mentoring, training, active listening, and self-discovery that there are a lot of other people out there who can get it done too, and, in truth, my way may not be the best way.

But creating close personal connections is part of my day-to-day work now. My original background is in accounting—I'm a CPA, a numbers person. I'm most comfortable sitting at a computer, working with data and spreadsheets to solve financial problems, but as CEO of my own company, I have to push myself out of my comfort zone and connect with my team for the good of the business and the people I value so much. A tool my husband, Mark, taught me a long ago is one I still try to use as often as possible: a morning walk-around. When the leader comes in first thing in the morning, they should take a few minutes to walk around and see how everyone is doing. Be genuine, and take the time, even if only ten minutes. Share a story of your personal life and what you are dealing with, whether kids, pets, or grandkids. It helps you and your team to connect to each other and drives home the concept of working together rather than working for you.

It hasn't been easy. I'm very hands-on, so when I take a long flight to Europe, Kuwait, or Southwest Asia—which I do fairly often—it can be difficult for me to put aside my daily tasks and reach out to team members and make those connections.

Of course, when I'm on those visits, I need to find out how business is going and how my team is performing, but just as important—maybe even more important—as I talk with our people, I'm looking them in the eye and getting feedback. Are they happy in their work? What are they truly concerned about? Can I help them solve a business problem? Do they want to share anything about their personal life (I'm a good listener)? I want them to know that, to me, they're not just workers; they're important, and I care about them.

Points to Ponder

1. In what ways can your organization practice informal leadership–do you see situations in which informal leaders can help and even excel with this different leadership attitude?

2. Are there people in your company who would be great informal leaders? What leadership attitude do they have that would make them excel at this?

3. What benefits do you hope to achieve by using informal leaders to guide and motivate team members?

4. Why do you think these informal leaders might have a different leadership attitude in your organization that could achieve better results than formal leaders with impressive-sounding job titles?

5. Would your organization benefit from providing training for informal leadership attitudes?

Chapter 7

A Glimpse into the Process

I love you, Lord, my strength. The Lord is my rock, my fortress and my
deliverer; my God is my rock, in whom I take refuge, my shield and
the horn of my salvation, my stronghold. I called to the Lord, who is
worthy of praise, and I have been saved from my enemies. The cords of
death entangled me; the torrents of destruction overwhelmed me. The
cords of the grave coiled around me; the snares of death confronted me.
In my distress I called to the Lord; I cried to my God for help. From his
temple he heard my voice; my cry came before him, into his ears.

———————————————————— —PSALM 18:1-6 ——————

P art of our footprint at PZI is collaboration, the human touch. We have plenty of remote employees—our people work all over the world. But our core group needs to be together. They need to be able to visit and work together in person, so there's just nothing like coming into the office. Once every quarter, we bring in several of our facilitators who work with us as faculty at Army University, as well as our accounting, Talent Globalization®, and business systems groups—and they love being in the office with everyone else. They love feeling like they're part of something so intimate and connected.

When everyone is together, we do simple things like provide water, sodas, coffee, snacks, and, of course, chocolate. After all, what we do is stressful. People come to us about stressful parts of their lives, whether it's relocating, or payroll, or learning new skill sets. But it's also exciting. Even though there are routines and set processes, we have different types of client companies coming and going all the time, so there is something new to learn every day. It's very fast-paced and never the same thing.

Our Growth

As I mentioned earlier, when I first started out, I was working in an entrepreneur incubator, and we were using the Huntsville Botanical Gardens for our training sessions. As the company grew, we took over seven offices at the incubator, at which point we were told that we had officially "graduated, we needed to move out," much like when you tell your children that it's time to leave the nest and fly. We decided to move into a space where the training center could be on-site and the working spaces would be open, enabling more collaboration. We moved into a four-thousand-square-foot office space with room for training around thirty people at a time. When we moved in, I told the landlords that I wanted first right of refusal if adjacent spaces ever opened up. Before long, we were using the training center to office some of our people, so as soon as adjacent offices opened up, we moved into those as well. Now we have a fourteen-thousand-square-foot office where the cubicles are only shoulder high so that you can see people's faces, and there's room for training around fifty people at a time.

As we continued to grow and divisions became companies, we would ultimately have seven companies. Seven is a special number. When you read through the Old Testament in the Bible, you will see that God did things in seven. Seven is God's number. The seven interconnected companies in PZI Group started out with PZI International Consulting, Inc., which was our initial consulting and workforce development company. Our second company, PZI International Solutions, Inc., a global employment solutions company started with the email that I ignored three times. Global employment is when you are employing people around the globe, in many different ways. We look at where the person is being sent: what contracts are needed, what are the requirements for transferring that person, what are the logistics of getting them from a location in the country they are to a new home in a new country? We relocate people, make sure they can speak the language, have benefit coverage when they get there, set up cultural training for them, deal with taxation, find them housing, and the list continues. Organizations spend millions of dollars on international assignments, so they don't want those employees (those assets) walking out the door. We also have to look at things like getting the employee excited about making the international change, moving their family, uprooting their life, coaching them through the many different pieces of it, and being there to listen to them and help guide them. We ensure they ask the right questions, and if they don't know what to ask, we do what we always do, which is to know the question they didn't even think of asking. We encourage them to be bold and adapt a new attitude in the organization, a leadership attitude.

After twenty-plus years in the industry, I was able to bring a large network with me to start PZI. PZI was built with that network of over two hundred established supplier relationships that I had established over time, and so, now, when companies need our help, they get the network and the intellectual capital.

Over time, we grew to the point of being able to open up our own company in the United Kingdom, then in Germany, Japan, Australia, and ultimately in thirty countries.

After the second company, PZI International Solutions, Inc., the next company that was established was Clark Global Institute. Clark Global Institute is named after my first grandson (Clark), my second grandson (Glenn), and my son (Ian). It came about because the organization I had been involved with from a training standpoint, during my corporate career, the National Foreign Trade Council (NFTC), had decided to dissolve an important function that it offered, International Assignment Management Committees, which was known as an international Human Resource Consulting group. That organization was composed of around three hundred companies made up of the global leads of multinational organizations' IHR and global mobility functions. Once every six months, these professionals would meet for three days to talk about policies, processes, vendors, best practices, and so on. That had been ongoing for about thirty years, but NFTC decided that it did not want to support IHR anymore; it just wanted to focus on imports, exports, controls, international trade regulation administration, and requirements.

I had received a great deal of value from being a member of a steering committee in the organization; in fact, I credit a lot of the skills I have to this organization and group. When the person who had been running it for more than a decade was let go, she and I met, and, during that conversation, she mentioned that someone should start a company to pick up where the NFTC group had left off. So, I hired her to design and run the company, and she put together everything we needed to approach all of the members who had been in the group so that we could keep it going. It was a big investment and took about six months to put together, but I wanted the value I had experienced by being a part of this group to benefit new IHR and mobility managers.

After we had all the programs, procedures, websites, and other pieces put together, we approached the previous members of the group and offered the service to them for a fee, which was needed to pay for salaries and for operating the program. But at that point, I was a vendor, which was something the members of the group did not want to deal with. So, I removed myself from the business day-to-day operations and only into the role of founder and owner. That would keep the corporate piece completely separate. We presented the company to the group, and about half of them were undecided or leaning toward another, larger organization that was going to put something together and offer certifications. Unfortunately, that never materialized. Today, Clark Global Institute provides workforce development and other trainings as a subcontractor to PZI International Consulting, Inc.

Next came PZI Business Systems Solutions (BSS). As my organization began to grow, I knew that I needed a data analytical tool that would help to manage the multitude of human resource information that was needed to run an international organization. We had outgrown our automated excel workbooks. I chose to work with a small development group out of New Jersey, Keypress Software Development Group, to help us develop our own Global HR Information System. This tool is known as Employee Global Logistics (EGL'). Not only is this used for our other global business entities, but we also license the tool to organizations to utilize it for their IHR management. With BSS, we review the processes of global organizations and look at quality control, process management, and other systems, to determine how they can best streamline and manage those processes. Often that is with the use of our software, and EGL is part of managing some of those systems. It's completely automated and system driven, in essence as complete international HR ecosystem. Our first client – a major government contractor with thousands of international employees and its own IHR team of nearly two dozen IHR, relocation and tax professionals—still utilizes our tool today.

The tool continues to grow in functionality and diversity. Today, we have brought all software development in house to continue growing EGL as well as other software solutions.

The relocation management part of the group is through PZI Talent Mobility Solutions™ (TMS), which was originally a part of PZI International Consulting, Inc. That corporation is a fully stand-alone relocation management outsourcing company providing full scope household goods relocation services, home sale assistance, housing options, and travel management, both domestically and internationally.

Understanding the complexities of international benefits is no small task. As I navigated this within large corporations, I was amazed to find how many domestic benefit brokers would broker international benefits but really didn't understand how they work and how best to advise their clients in this complex environment. So I decided to obtain my insurance broker license, along with my certified public accounting license, to be able to help our clients with this needed piece of "fiduciary duty of care" for their international employees. That became another company, PZI International Benefits Brokerage Solutions, where we offer health, wellness, and ancillary benefits for our global clients.

Working with Clients

While our clients are corporations, it's actually the people in those corporations whom we're serving: the HR group and director, the tax group and director, the payroll group and director, not to mention the employee and the employee's family. Someone has reached out to PZI because they have a problem. They've been given a task, but they're not sure what to do. They know a little bit about us. They may have found us on our website, www.PZIconsulting.com, or somebody's told them to give us a call because we can help with their problem, and we're always the organization with the out-of-the-box solutions. When we say, "Sure, we can help with that," it isn't because we are consultants; we ensure we can help solve problems. *We support people*—that's our mission, and it's a simple, Christian directive.

When clients come to us, they have a problem, a business need, a human need. Maybe they need a new contract, or they have a new opportunity, but they're not sure how to go about it, and they aren't sure how to get the right talent to that incredible opportunity. We talk with them about their issues, their problems, and then we find solutions. We really are problem-solvers. We usually start by asking them what they are currently doing and what they like and don't like about their current situation. We want to know their pain points; we want them to talk about themselves. Then we use our active listening skills because their real problem is not always apparent; sometimes we discover it just from a little story or a tidbit that they share. Maybe it's around recruitment, maybe retention. It might be around legal setup or behaviors. Sometimes we find the answers to questions that clients didn't even know to ask.

But it's always about people. That's why we say we're people first. We are about supporting people adapt and connect. Whether it's payroll, accounting, benefits, relocation, workforce development, anything we do, we're connecting with a person, and we're connecting that person to something. That feeling of supporting someone—there's nothing better for the soul. It's like being the hands and feet of Jesus; we're that human connection in a time of need.

Solving People Problems

We get clients from all kinds of situations, and when we meet with them to start troubleshooting, it's often either in the office or virtual. As I mentioned, we sometimes find out that their real problem is not apparent; it's something we didn't know about when we may have come to see them for another reason. Sometimes we have to pivot, just like Jesus did. He was always pivoting, always putting the lesson back on whomever he was with. That's what happened with one group recently.

We were hired to conduct workforce development training for a small group of people, a two-day session on team effectiveness, serious executive-level stuff. When we were there, we realized that what was really needed was an intervention with the group. There was extreme dislike within the team. They wouldn't talk to one another; they wouldn't even look at one another. Skill-wise, they were all extremely well suited for what was needed, but they could not get past their own behavioral biases, making it impossible to move forward in what was already a very high-stress situation.

We at first thought we could start at a high level and then drill down into the issues, but then we quickly realized that we needed to throw out everything and start over. We had to make the team uncomfortable and get into the issues. It definitely got intense, but at the end of the second day, the leader commented that it was the best training the team had ever had. That was evident by the fact that the team was able to finally get past their barriers and begin connecting with one another and making a difference in one another's lives.

Being able to adapt and connect and pick up on what people are actually saying or doing, or what they mean, often based on their behaviors, can make all the difference in moving forward.

Let God—and Others—Get the Mission Done

Maybe it's because of my connections to the business world that I keep seeing so many similarities as I read the Bible, but to me, it's so clear: whether it was thousands of years ago or modern day, at their cores, people really haven't changed a whole lot over the years. Behaviors may have changed a little, and circumstances definitely have changed, but we're still doing the same things. Yes, cultures are different around the world, and those cultures have an influence on how a person is brought up, what they think, and how they act. In the United States alone, there are differences in regions. Someone from New Jersey may be very straightforward, even blunt, whereas someone from Georgia may use charm to get their way—both people may be after the same thing, but they just come at it differently.

During the episode I just explained, we discovered that the core of the problem was with two key individuals who simply did not gel. They did not like one another, but they had to work together. Solving the problem required us to come out of our rehearsed place to connect, and that required some vulnerability on our part because we had to use our own insecurities, our own stories to get the others to see that we're all alike so they felt comfortable opening up. So I brought up a time when I, as the CEO, had an issue where my right-hand person, my second-in-command, was not committed to the mission—the person did not agree on where I knew the company needed to go. After I explained that scenario to the group, I asked them, "What would you do in this situation?" Then I stayed silent and let each person in the group talk. I didn't necessarily need their advice on what I should have done in that situation. I knew what I needed to do about it. But by letting each person on the team talk about that scenario—a situation outside their own— they were able to see what was really going on in their own group. What was interesting was that each person talked about coaching, working together, exploring the issues, and finding solutions—none of them said, "Get rid of the second-in-command." It was clear that they wanted the situation to work. When I pointed out to the team that not one of them had said, "Fire that person," as the solution, it was a lightbulb for them. That's when they realized that they really did want their team to succeed.

Interestingly, I normally would not even have been part of that training, but I wanted to work with that particular client, and when we saw what was happening, I knew that God wanted me to be there, and he helped me know just what to say.

Training through Discomfort

A part of what we do at PZI is train informal leaders through attitudes of influence. When it comes to training informal leaders, a lot of what we do is put people in uncomfortable situations so that they have to practice what to do. It might be for something as small as changing who leads the next meeting or who prepares a PowerPoint. Even if someone else does it better, others need to try so that they can learn. Sometimes people are intimidated by others that they think are better, but they got better because they practiced. Nobody is an expert the first time they try something; it takes practice, and it takes failure. I tell my staff often, "I didn't get where I was by not making mistakes. It's the only way to learn the hard, never-do-it-again type of leadership attitudes."

When I created the High 5!° Program, which is our five levels of behavioral leadership training, I created it to address the supervisor-employee connection and the attitude supervisors and employees bring with them in these relationships. I created the program because I feel that, if we can get to supervisors early in their careers instead of after they had been in the workforce for thirty years, then maybe we will be coaching executives on their legacies rather than their behaviors. If we can help them understand their behaviors and how to change their attitudes to adapt and connect earlier in their careers, then they can become a leader that people will actually want to follow, and they will be practiced at being an executive when they step into their higher roles. In the program, we try to help leaders learn to lead by picking up on and adapting to others' preferences. The Golden Rule is, "Do unto others as you have them do unto you." But that's treating people the way *you* want to be treated, and they're not you. So we say, "Do unto others as they would be done unto." Figure out how they need to be connected to and what their behaviors are because you can't change other people; you can only change yourself.

In our informal leadership course that we lead as part of Army University faculty, we work with informal leaders for the US Army Command Team Spouse Development Program–Battalion (CTSDP-BN), emulating techniques for conflict resolution and situational leadership. We work with this group for command spouses in the military because even while their spouse is a formal leader as a commander, the spouse at home is typically involved in some way, in an informal leadership role. These spouses may not have rank or title or job description, and no one is required to follow them, but they have definite roles, nonetheless. It's up to them to know how to be an informal leader, to have a leadership attitude, to be able to resolve conflicts in a professional way, to be able to help family members in their organization go from their late teen years as someone who doesn't even know how to balance a bank account to being married with kids and their spouse is gone for a month at a time. Those are things that the US Army is not going to take care of, but those are the realities of the situation where these informal leaders are put into, and we help train through those difficult situations and ensure their leadership attitude is the best it can be.

For government agencies and corporations, we also work on leadership attitudes with informal leadership situations. For instance, we have a program called Influencing Up through our PZI workforce development group, which facilitates how to exhibit the characteristics of a giving leadership attitude and how to influence a situation when you don't have a title. In this program, we have some fun as well, by using difficult scenarios in various settings, even in an escape room, high-stress environment.

One of the most difficult leadership decisions is to know when someone is ready for the formal leadership role. Leadership is more than a bigger office, higher pay, more responsibility, and a title; it has to be enveloped in the attitude of the new leader. This is where we so often fail our new leaders, by promoting them because of the great technical skill level they have but without teaching them how to be a great leader, which is a completely different skill set. Leadership skills are not like technical skills, where you "learn it on the job." That's where organizations lose their best employees to a new leader who didn't really understand that their role was to be a servant and not a "boss."

We also help clients better understand how to know when someone is ready for a leadership role and how much time and effort to invest in someone's development. This is an issue I've dealt with at PZI: I have seen people who should be leading but were afraid to take the next step because of being denied opportunities in previous roles. I saw that in one employee and gave her an opportunity to move up because she was so competent. I told her that we would support her in the move, but she felt she wasn't ready. A year later, she was; she realized others were passing her by and that it was time for her to become the person that she needed to be. I'm blessed that I was given the opportunity to keep her in the organization, to allow her that time to grow until she was ready to take that step, because sometimes there just isn't enough time to wait.

Again, it's all about getting people out of their comfort zone. In our workforce development training, we don't allow participants to sit more than about ten to fifteen minutes. We want them out of their chairs, role-playing in unfamiliar settings, doing something actionable. It's really about practice; if we can get them to go through a situation—to practice it—during a training session, then they'll be more comfortable trying it in a familiar setting.

Points to Ponder

1. When working with members of the team or clients, are you actively listening to what they have to say? More than just asking them about their current situation, are you asking them about what they like— and don't like—about the situation that they are in? Are you sure what you are saying is what they are hearing?

2. In what ways are you training through discomfort? How are you getting your team out of their comfort zones to learn new insights about their roles and themselves?

3. Are you and your team able to manage through the most difficult conversations? How does that look for you and your team so that everyone comes out intact and in a better place than when they went in?

4. How are you being the hands and feet of Jesus? In what way are you serving your team, your clients, your community?

5. How is your leadership attitude toward showing your organization that you care for them and want to connect?

6. Is your mission about helping others or helping yourself? Are you committed to being a servant leader instead of being a served leader?

Chapter 8

The Military Component

Now Deborah, a prophet, the wife of Lappidoth, was leading Israel at that time.... She sent for Barak son of Abinoam from Kedesh in Naphtali and said to him, "The Lord, the God of Israel, commands you: 'Go, take with you ten thousand men of Naphtali and Zebulun and lead them up to Mount Tabor. I will lead Sisera, the commander of Jabin's army, with his chariots and his troops to the Kishon River and give him into your hands.'" Barak said to her, "If you go with me, I will go; but if you don't go with me, I won't go." "Certainly I will go with you," said Deborah. "But because of the course you are taking, the honor will not be yours, for the Lord will deliver Sisera into the hands of a woman."

—JUDGES 4:4, 6–9

B ecause I am a female entrepreneur with a military affiliation background, I have always been very passionate about giving military spouses and females an opportunity when I can. Today, around 85 percent of the PZI workforce is made up of military spouses and veterans. I feel it's important to give back some of what I was able to enjoy during my husband's thirty-one years in the military. Large corporate organizations took a chance on me, and I try to pay that forward. While military affiliation and gender are certainly a core focus, what we're really focusing on are people who want to be a part of the overall team and move our mission of supporting others forward. If a team member is concerned only about themselves and not about the team first, I know it is not going to work out, no matter what gender or military affiliation they have.

One person who epitomizes what we're working to achieve is Michelle Nash, who was originally hired as an hourly paid facilitator and has moved through the organization to now be our vice president of human resources and workforce development. She started working with us, while her spouse was still on active-duty service in the military. At the time, Michelle was the leader of the Military Council of Catholic Women-Worldwide (MCCW). It was a big job in which she managed thirty volunteers on a global basis and reported to the Archdiocese for the Military Services (AMS), USA. A mutual acquaintance introduced us when I was helping an organization with cultural transformation. Our mutual acquaintance thought I could help Michelle with some issues she was having with her own team. I invited her to attend one of our classes to see firsthand what we were doing and whether it might be helpful. She knew right away that she wanted us to come and help her.

She asked me to come to the organization's annual retreat. Because this was a nonprofit, it really didn't have funds for providing individual assessments or professional development for volunteer staff. I reached out to Insights Discovery˚, one of our largest suppliers, which had a nonprofit program called Gifts of Discovery that could assist in providing the assessments, free of charge, for up to thirty participants, to present it at the retreat. At the annual retreat, PZI gave a four-hour facilitation to the group along with the personal assessments. It made such a huge impact on Michelle's team that the organization started seeing immediate change. The volunteer members started connecting and adapting to one another's communication styles, and the needs of the organization were met quickly and efficiently—so much so that Michelle's role as lead organizer was no longer needed. She literally worked herself out of a job. That's the job of a great leader, when they can make such an impact that the organization can run without them. So Michelle, a professional volunteer, approached me about volunteering with PZI. I quickly let her know that PZI is a for-profit organization and she couldn't volunteer for us, but she could work for us as a part-time intern. Since I wasn't making a lot of money back then, she came on as an intern to learn a few things in a shadowing role.

Insights Discovery˚ is a personality assessment tool that we utilize at PZI. I utilized this tool when I was working in large corporations, and I ended up using it in ten different languages. The corporate sales representative for the tool was persistent; he kept coming back to me for probably six months, and I kept turning him away thinking it wasn't the right fit for what I do. One day I just happened to pick up the phone, and there was the representative, urging me to just try the assessment myself for free. Finally, I agreed, but I didn't really take it seriously. At the time, I had taken over ten assessment tools in my career and really didn't see how another one could possibly make any difference. After agreeing to take it, I completely forgot about it, until one morning when I took it while I was getting ready for work. It took about ten minutes; I didn't give it a lot of thought afterward because I was only doing it as a "favor." But it made such an impactful change on how I saw myself that I agreed to try it on my corporate team at that time. Seeing how it worked on my team, and then how we utilized it within the organization with hundreds of individuals in many different languages, I knew this was not a normal tool. It is the only one I even considered bringing with me as a possible workforce development tool when I started PZI. Now we use it regularly at PZI along with other assessment tools and curriculum that we have developed as well. We've done thousands of assessments with it because it's a very powerful tool. We like it because it's very actionable and easy to quickly understand and utilize for immediate impact.

As Michelle was interning with us and helping at workshops, an opportunity came open that I like to think was a "God Wink" moment. I had a new individual lined up to come to work for us as a licensed facilitator, but they had to go through the weeklong training for the curriculum. The individual called me a week before the program was to begin to say they were turning down the opportunity after all. When Michelle heard about it, she immediately said, "I'll do it." Although I had great respect for Michelle, she was an active-duty military wife who had spent the last twenty years volunteering, not working in a corporate job, and had always followed her spouse as his career progressed. Investing in her, not knowing whether she would be able to stay with PZI for more than a year, was a big leap of faith for me. Having been in that military spouse role myself for more than thirty years, I knew that it would be very tough to manage the volunteer role with a working corporate role. In many cases, a military spouse's role is really what I call a "professional volunteer" role; that's the "role" many military spouses take on after leaving a career to follow their soldier and be the boots on the ground for the family members in a unit. That "professional volunteer" role requires many skills and, in some ways, is actually harder than a corporate role. You have to recruit other volunteers, motivate them, develop them, and manage them, all without any financial resources or promise of advancement. It's a role that is often viewed as not having much value, although I knew exactly how much value someone with those skills would be worth in any organization. Often, these professional volunteers come to feel that they don't have skills that would make them employable. But with Michelle, for instance, she had been designing and running large organizations for years that had budgets consisting of hundreds of thousands of dollars and hundreds of volunteer staff. One of her best leadership attitudes is getting people to want to work for and with her.

I decided to give her the opportunity and send her through the facilitator training course, where she received her certification, and then started working for PZI. It was slow going at first; she only worked around fifteen hours a week for the first three months. But as her role started to gel and she became more comfortable with the curriculum and her new skill set, she became such a phenomenal facilitator that another facilitator left the organization after feeling somewhat threatened by all of Michelle's energy and enthusiasm for her role. Finally, Michelle went full-time, and, today, she does it all: designs curriculum, trains new facilitators, coaches, develops processes, facilitates courses, and most importantly, guides the culture of servant leadership at PZI. She's a real cheerleader for this organization and has even been my faith mentor. When things get chaotic, she reminds me, "Hey, Debbie, this is all God; this is his plan. Stop worrying about it." Interestingly, she even pointed out to me that we met through GOD, an abbreviation for the Gifts of Discovery training opportunity.

"I Thirst Thursday"

At PZI, everything we do includes Christian values. And as I've mentioned, Michelle is a key part of that. She keeps me faithful and focused; we often joke that I'm her Deborah and she's my Jaelle.

Every Thursday, Michelle hosts the "I Thirst Thursday" podcast, which is about how Jesus shows up in certain words and how we use those words. As part of the podcast, Michelle chooses a word of the week and then discusses how that word is used in a Christian way. The podcast is based on John 4, where Jesus meets the Samaritan woman at the well. At the time, Samaritans were viewed as great sinners because they were separated from Israel, idolized pagan gods, and married pagans; for Jesus to spend time with such an impure woman was appalling to some but not to Jesus. Instead, he sought to meet her where she was at that particular moment in time. That's what he does for all of us—and that's what we try to do at PZI. We meet organizations where they are and help them to the next step.

The Military and Me

My husband, Mark, and I did not come from military backgrounds. We both grew up in small southern towns, with the same background. We both went to the same school for most of our lives and had the same friends through a majority of our formative years. I met Mark when I was a senior in high school and he was a sophomore at the local college. Going into the military was really a financial decision and, at first, was something of a shock. Mark's dad was a big believer in taking responsibility for your actions, so shortly after we got married, he took Mark aside and said, "Son, if you are old enough to have a wife, you are old enough to pay for your own school." And with that, we became financially independent. It started with Mark entering the Army National Guard, which wasn't full-time active duty but only one weekend a month and two weeks in the summer. The plan was that I would work full-time while he was in college, and then when he graduated, I would go to college. The military was not in our "plans." But pretty early on, Mark was identified as a candidate for military officer candidate school (OCS). He graduated first in his class in the OCS, and the Army offered him active-duty status as a second lieutenant. He hadn't even finished his college degree, and I hadn't started mine, when he called me up and asked what I thought about going into to see the world for around five or six years. We were young, twenty and twenty-one, and thought we would see the world for a few years and then come back and continue life as we had planned. But God had a different plan. Thirty-one years and twenty-two moves later, Mark retired as a full-bird colonel. The military lifestyle was not in my plan, but it was a good fit for us and our family, and I grew and matured during our time in the military.

Our first post was in Fort Riley, Kansas. I was twenty years old and had been married for three years already, and Mark was a second lieutenant. But because of the liquor laws back then (you had to be twenty-one to drink even wine or beer in Kansas), I could not even buy a bottle of wine for guests when we were having a small dinner party. It was a stark realization that you had to be flexible and adapt quickly in your environment, whatever or wherever that might be.

Even at seventeen, I had known I wanted to be a CPA, so I never gave up trying to obtain my education. Every state we moved to required a year's residency before granting in-state tuition at their universities. When you're someone who moves every year or two, that's tough to accomplish. After seven years, and five different universities, I finally earned my undergraduate accounting degree. By this time, Mark was a major; we'd been in the military for more than a decade and had two of our three boys. I knew I would sit for the CPA exam, and at this time, you only needed an undergraduate accounting degree to sit for that exam. Since it was such an ordeal to obtain the undergraduate degree and pass the CPA exam, moving from state to state, that I decided not to pursue my master's degree.

After finishing college, we had our third son and moved, six months later, to a new state. Mark was pretty tired of me actually going to school for so long and offered me a deal: If I got a job, we would take the money and go on a cruise. We would only be in the new location for one year, so it wasn't likely that I'd even be able to find a company willing to hire me, but I gave it a shot.

That's how my career started. I went to work for Arthur Andersen as a staff auditor, in Overland Park, Kansas, an opportunity that opened up doors for me forever. Although I was only there for one year, it would be an opportunity that would open more doors for me shortly after leaving Kansas. We spent another two years in Virginia, but Arthur Andersen was not in the city where we lived, so I worked for a small CPA firm instead. When Mark received orders to move to a new station in Germany after Virginia, I contacted Arthur Anderson back in Kansas to inquire about any opportunities in Germany. The partner connected with a colleague of his in Germany, and an opportunity to work in Frankfurt, but in a different accounting role, was made available to me.

I would go from an auditor to an international taxation staff accountant. I had to take a demotion and a cut in pay, but I learned an entirely new skill set, and it was the start of my international career.

Three months into this new duty station and new job, the Army deployed Mark for a year. That was before FaceTime and cell phones, so we communicated by writing letters and, a few times a week, exchanging emails (through the old-time dial-up service). Over twelve months, we had a handful of phone calls and a two-week home visit. That was it. Like most military spouses, we simply learned how to "get it done." It was up to me to manage the household, the funds, the kids, and a job. One day, my senior partner at Andersen came to me and told me he didn't know how I was able to do a full-time job and a full-time single-parent situation in a foreign country, so he offered the availability of going to a three-day workweek. This was long before remote work was even an option. Working with a company like that, with not only a caring boss but also the availability of career enhancement, meant the world to me. I ensured the time I put into the three-day workweek was as productive as a five-day workweek. The shorter workweek also gave me the downtime to manage the military volunteer and family side of my life. Working with this international company allowed me the ability to pretty much write my own ticket in the industry, and that opportunity led to more opportunities throughout my career. Later, Mark was relocated to Fort Bliss in El Paso, Texas, and while Andersen did not have a presence in El Paso, another Big Four accounting firm, KPMG did. I was not planning to work full-time because Mark had agreed to take a command position, so I thought I would just manage some volunteer activities as a military spouse and not work. But the opportunity that was presented to me by KPMG was for a manager to run its Mexico-US individual tax practice. Since I had experience from Germany with expatriate taxation, the firm hired me as the full-time manager for its Maquiladora practice.

Over time, I was afforded similar opportunities from other employers, and I did my best to not let them down—that's why I want to give that same opportunity to team members through PZI.

Not Social Calendar Keepers

Throughout it all, I had to rely on other relationships, Christian relationships, which are huge in the military. Every military unit has a chaplain assigned to it; there were Catholic and Protestant Women of the Chapel organizations and open prayers before events to give thanks for the blessing we received—everything was about God and country and duty. Those are in the oaths that the military active duty personnel take, but ones we agree to as well, as the spouses who support and follow. It's a mission for a military family, not a job. There's a lot of self-sacrifice and servant leadership ingrained in military spouses and families from the very beginning of a career; without those customs and practices, many military spouses would not be very successful.

Still, a military spouse is not just a social calendar keeper. They are informal leaders in their volunteer positions, even though they often are not given any significant resources or specific training for their inferred role. Their leadership attitude must be one of servant-hood and a true desire to make things better for their organization and their family while at this new station.

Early on, as a military spouse, the Army offered me some professional training as an Army Family Team Builder. It was good training and information, but still really focused on traditional roles and responsibilities; it was not the kind of leadership training I would go through as a corporate team member and manager. There has not traditionally been funding allocated toward the volunteer side of the military, although in the last ten years, that does seem to be changing. When Mark and I first entered the military community in 1979, the Army was coming out of the post-draft era and the Vietnam War. The regard for US military members was not high in our civilian society, and I think many facets of that era took a long time to recover. When Desert Storm happened in 1992, it was the first time the military was actually going to "war" since the end of the Vietnam era. The continually training mindset that was the operations of the military sector during the Cold War was about to change, and then after the 9/11 attacks, the entire world changed as well as the military focus. The operational tempo that was much slower for us as young military servicemen and military families was no longer the operational tempo that the post-9/11 families would face.

There had not traditionally been much funding devoted to informal leadership and the role of the family member, other than a "team builder." Yet when a service member is given a battalion command, it's a major shift in leadership attitudes. The military member commands anywhere from a few hundred to nearly a thousand service members. When there's an accompanying spouse, often that spouse is put into an informal leadership position within the command structure that might be as simple as fundraising or something much more complex, such as deployment family and team support/logistics.

For instance, when the airplane struck the Pentagon during the 9/11 attacks, Mark was in the Pentagon. The plane stopped about a hundred feet from his office. At the time, we had been in Washington, DC, only for two months, just out of a stressful two years of battalion command, and the country was not at war. I was working with KPMG in Tyson's Corner and on the phone with a client when a colleague came into my office and told me I needed to get off the phone—*now*. At first, I didn't realize the seriousness of his tone, but I ended my call with the client. Then my colleague told me what happened. The phones were out of order everywhere, so I couldn't reach Mark. My colleague quickly drove me home, and then I quietly reverted into military spouse and mom mode training, which I had been privileged to learn earlier. I systematically went to each of the schools to pick up my kids and got them home, and then I began to start the normal military logistics spouse mode of contacting individual family members within the unit. We call this the "phone tree." I was able to reach Mark's direct supervisor's spouse, who was a colonel's wife (Mark was a lieutenant colonel at the time), and we made our way through the contact tree and the individuals we knew about and as many people as we could get in touch with. We started going down the list: Who worked in what office? Where is their spouse right now? How do we get in touch with them? What is their phone number? Those are the kinds of things that come naturally to a military spouse, in time of crisis, as I had been "informally trained" for years in it. It was another seven hours before I heard from Mark, but I consider myself extremely blessed because my husband came home that day.

While my career path did not take me down the role of full-time military spouse team member, there are others who do take on that role and do an excellent job at it. For instance, Mark likes to say, "The military is two hundred years of tradition, unimpeded by progress." At a formal military function, there is often a receiving line. There is a definite logistical system of these receiving lines, and it is usually structured by a rank of the military member. Sometimes the military member is there; other times, only the spouse of the military member is there representing their spouse's position. Whatever the situation, the military spouse has their spot in that line. I was reminded of that after standing in the wrong "spot" at a function—I was quickly corrected by one of the full-time military spouses whose informal career revolved around their spouse's formal role. These informal leaders take their duty to their spouse, the military, and the organization very seriously. I thank God for those spouses, and they have earned the right to move someone out of their spot. The service member and their military spouse are the people who let others not in the military sleep well at night.

But that was not the role I chose. Mark and I made a decision early in our lives that I would always focus on a career that would serve us as a family, after his military career was finished. And I managed to juggle it all because I've always been someone who thinks out of the box; doing things off the beaten path is part of my DNA. That served me well in a culture that requires flexibility. Service members and their families relocate often; every six months to three years they are uprooted and sent where they are needed. But it's also part of the service member's development. In the Army, the average age is twenty-six. There are a lot of deployments and a lot of burnout. But knowing that your situation will change in a short period of time helps with the burnout and keeps fresh ideas and different ways of doing things on a continual basis. You're trained and schooled for different skill sets based on the position, the need, the installation, and the mission. You have a lot of different jobs and different supervisors but one employer throughout it all—very different from the corporate world.

In fact, the military has always been the great experiment for the American culture because it is an isolated culture within the US culture that has its own set of rules and operational guidelines that work in conjunction with the rest of civilian society. If there is a need to change something in the American society, often it is tried out in the US military first. Examples include women in a new role (combat-related, pilots, first women in a military academy), segregation, desegregation, African American pilots—they try it out in the military first to see what works and what doesn't. That's because these are people who are great at solving problems and finding solutions—ideal traits for PZI.

Military and PZI

When I started the company, I can't honestly say military spouses were on my radar as potential employees. I knew what I was looking for in an employee, but I couldn't really find it, and I had a lot of turnover in the first few years. Since I was new to the area where PZI is headquartered, client contacts just didn't exist for me.

In fact, Michelle, whose story I told at the beginning of the chapter, was the first military spouse whom we hired. In part, because of the phenomenal job that she has done, we started really looking at skill sets when hiring, not just past roles. Too often, their skill sets are downplayed or overlooked, with the "volunteer experience" caveat. I saw that in myself; I have a hard time recognizing things that I've done as a volunteer military spouse because that's part of the servant leadership mentality that is just ingrained from a very early age within the military culture.

But again, we really look at skill sets when we hire at PZI. For instance, we are part of the Department of Defense Military Spouse Employment Partnership (MSEP). We also work with Hiring Our Heroes program and recently hired seven spouses from that program. Some of the skill sets that make military members and their spouses such a valuable asset to any organization include the ability to pivot from one task to another task quickly, being able to think out-of-the-box solutions, being able to problem-solve without direction, not needing constant oversight, and being able to stand on your own two feet and figure it out, all while verbalizing or documenting the solutions for your supervisors to understand. Those skill sets work very well at PZI.

Individuals in the military are used to being given a lot of autonomy to figure out solutions and become leaders. There's always a formal leader, a chain of command, but there are many informal leaders in the ranks. That's what military spouses are: they have no direct authority militarily, so they must learn how to lead without rank. They must utilize their skill sets to show people that they are there to serve, to be part of the team, to help make others' lives better.

Those who are good at it make phenomenal team members at PZI. They just automatically know how to identify a problem and find a solution for it without being told a solution or prodded to come up with one. And, as informal leaders, their leadership attitude is they care about the person and the task; they do things because they care and want to be part of something important. That's when that servant leadership attitude really comes out.

The Changing Role

Since I was so fortunate to maintain a career while also being an involved military spouse, I'm determined that we will give opportunities to these same types of individuals whom I consider heroes. When you're a trailing military spouse, it's very hard to have a career, especially a fast-paced business career. When I was relocating those twenty-two times with Mark's career, I didn't always have a job waiting for me; I had to go find them. Rarely was I fortunate to have a transfer in line for me when my spouse had to transfer. I had to go find it. That means you have to get very good at always selling your attributes very well and be good at networking. It also means being open, transparent, and up-front with potential employers about your longevity and where your priorities are. For me, that meant I was only going to be there two years; I had children whom I was responsible for, often as a single parent, so I might only be able to work while they were in school; and I probably wasn't going to work fifty hours a week, at least not where they would physically see me. But I would be a team member who would dedicate all of the available time and energy to the company while I was there.

Through PZI, we're starting to help direct small changes in the role of military spouses by making it possible for these individuals to have a career and still fulfill their military spouse objectives, if they so choose. For starters, we recently hired six people from the MSEP program who are working all over the world. We're also currently the third-largest employer for the Military Spouse Employment Fellowship Pilot program, which is a paid fellowship program where military spouses can apply for placement with civilian companies who are seeking full-time employees. This program was put into place, much like the Hiring Our Heroes program, for active-duty military members transitioning out of their military careers.

The informal leadership program—the CTSDP-BN that we facilitate with Army University as part of its faculty—is another venue where we are helping to shape new leadership attitudes. The US Army has many training courses for its commanders and military personnel. When a service member enters battalion or brigade command, the service member usually has two or three weeks of strategy, organizational, and functionary training. In the past, the spouses joined the training for one of the weeks because they were viewed as part of the command team, and the military wanted to ensure that they understood the methodology and the culture of the battalion or brigade command for the next two years. When Mark was selected to go through this training as part of his battalion and brigade command prework, the spousal training was very traditionally based; what do you need to know to be a senior leader's spouse? What types of functions should you be attending? What are you responsible for in the way of social etiquette, invitations, and rank? Who do you need to know? Mostly, the role the spouse had been delegated to for many years. Since I had been fortunate to have many corporate leadership courses as part of my professional career, I knew what an organization was looking for in their formal and informal leaders and what the leadership attitude they wanted to cultivate was really all about.

When Michelle Nash and I identified the CTSDP-BN training program on the Government Services Administration's schedule, we thought it must be the same thing we had gone through as senior command team spouses, and we wanted to somehow be a part of it. We wanted to help drive change if we could. The faculty at Army University knew that the spousal role in the command team was changing, and the training offered to them as part of that command team needed to change as well. The course had always been taught with a lot of mentors and was a heavy volunteer organization. But the organization was looking to bring in a professional workforce development organization that could help them with that vision. We knew that PZI was the perfect fit for this because we had the same passion and commitment to mission that Army University had. We wanted today's spousal members to have the same professional career leadership training that PZI gave to corporations—the same kind of training I had done in my corporate professions. I wanted to be able to bring that to them, and that's what Army University was looking for too. It was looking for a way to bring a shift in leadership attitude for informal leadership training—which is such an important piece of the leadership for the military member—to the spouse. But how could that be done when the spouse has no direct authority?

It was and still is called spouse development instead of leadership training because, from a military standpoint, the spouse is the supporter, not the formal leader. It had been in years past much about understanding military protocols and tradition and how to organize a phone tree—all important things to know. But today, when more military spouses are working professionals and have master's degrees, like their service member spouse, the traditional training wasn't enough. This is what we hear from the trainees as well.

So, I decided if we were fortunate enough to be awarded the program, I wanted PZI to be the catalyst to work alongside Army University to embrace its vision and change the training program so that command team spouses could be trained as the professionals that they truly are. I wanted them to know more than just how to run a support group or a volunteer roster or set the table appropriately. I wanted them to get the informal leadership that could shift their leadership attitude and help them in their role as command team support as a military spouse, the same level of leadership training that is given to Army officers and noncommissioned officers.

We developed the program in conjunction with what Army University wanted: an informal leadership course with conflict resolution and situational leadership programs that would assist in shifting leadership attitude from supporter to informal leader. We made our proposal, which included trained and licensed instructors who were active or retired military spouses, because we wanted that empathy to be able to connect. But we insisted that we would not discuss our military spouse command background unless we were asked because it is strictly a professional leadership training, and we facilitate it the same way we would facilitate to the service members or a corporation. We ensure that we meet the mission that our clients lay out for us.

We did get the contract award, and today, it also includes self-awareness assessments as part of the program, using the Insights Discovery° tool that I previously mentioned. The assessment focuses on personal accountability for behaviors, and the program involves a lot of role play, which gives participants a safe environment to practice that behavioral change. They learn the importance of relationships for enhancing the team—what that looks like and how to walk and talk it. They leave having practiced enough and having learned how to be transparent and show vulnerability as a leader, which are important components of the leadership attitude that many leaders believe they should never show. Participants become more comfortable utilizing their new common language and helping facilitate their direct groups in shifting their leadership attitude as well. The situational leadership program that we use is Ken Blanchard's SLII°; in this program, participants go through different processes to identify different areas of support and leading. The program delves into understanding where a person is at a specific moment in time, helping to lead them in the situation they are in, and enabling them to grow into the more advanced competent team member in that task. The conflict leadership training that we provide uses the Thomas-Kilmann Instrument (TKI) system.

We use a lot of different systems and develop our own curriculum for all of our programs and clients that we work with, including the Army University programs. We tweak the programs for the mission needs to ensure we accomplish the shift in attitude of the participants that the clients are looking for.

When we began the courses, several hundred battalion commanders came through the formal leadership program for their new roles, but there were only sixteen spouses in attendance for the spousal development program. Now, around seventy spouses come to each session offered. In today's military, there are many joint spouse commanders as well as working professionals. Having the active-duty military member, which may also be a spouse commander, is a definite game changer. They learn not only how to shift their leadership attitude when in the support role but also how to shift their leadership role when they are in their formal leadership role. This command program is so important to the US Army that the general who is the chief of staff and the sergeant major of the US Army attend a session with these three-hundred-plus commanders each month the training is taught at Army University Combined Arms School. To me, that is the pinnacle of showing up for your team. When the top tier takes time out of their schedule to come and talk to these individuals and their spouses about the importance of their role and the impact they will make to the young service members and families they lead, that is truly leading from the front. That's what more corporations should do for their new leaders; it makes an impact that is never forgotten in that new leader's attitude and can make an impact in many of their direct reports.

Faith to Overcome the Unknowns

The military background also works well at PZI because it's such a faith-based organization. Chaplains in the military always approach their role from a very inclusive perspective, because there are a lot of different faiths in the military. But it all boils down to putting faith in God because there are so many unknowns in the military. Service members are deployed at a moment's notice, and sometimes there isn't even enough time to alert the spouse: you don't know where they are, what's going on, when they're coming home. Even those in the military who are not of the Christian faith can feel its influence because putting your faith in something you cannot see but can feel is so strong. That feeling of faith and inclusivity helps here at PZI, where we sometimes stop to pray before meetings, events, or when presenting a big proposal to a client. We bring the strength of Christ into everything we do.

In my corporate days, I kept my profession and my personal life extremely separate. Sometimes people didn't even know I had a military background or was someone with deep faith. But at PZI, I'm able to exercise my passion for both, and I think some of that transparency is why we've been so successful.

I'm very proud of the mission the US military carries out and of my family's role in the mission; I'm very proud of what we, as a family and as an organization, have done to serve our country. And that's why so much of our workforce has a military base in some way, shape, or form. When you walk into my office, there is a World War II picture that one of my sons acquired during one of his command training stations. To me, it represents who we are: victory, coming home, success, family. And that military connection has contributed to my ability now to feel more comfortable being a transparent leader.

Points to Ponder

1. How are you establishing the mission in your organization? In what ways are you making the workday more than just a job for employees?

2. How are you acknowledging and utilizing the skill sets, not just the job history, of the members of your team? What opportunities are they given to shine as servant leaders?

3. How are you, as a leader, being transparent with your team? How are you showing them your authentic self?

Chapter 9

Lead with Your Heart and Help Others

Jesus called them together and said, "You know that the rulers of the Gentiles lord it over them, and their high officials exercise authority over them. Not so with you. Instead, whoever wants to become great among you must be your servant, and whoever wants to be first must be your slave—just as the Son of Man did not come to be served, but to serve, and to give his life as a ransom for many."

——————————— —MATTHEW 20:25-28 ———————————

International human capital solutions is all about supporting
people. When I was in Asia in my prior corporate job supporting
people. , one of the vice presidents of human resources told me that
it made sense for me to run the organization's IHR function because
I was a female and that function was about nurturing employees (I let
him know that 64 percent of all heads of HR are male, not female).
Well, more than just being a female, I've always been someone who
has tried to support other people. That's a mission I've been driven
by early in my life, from my Christian Southern Baptist upbringing
to my early twenties as a military spouse, and I just brought that into
the business. Early in my career, I wasn't really that way, probably to
my detriment. As a product of the way previous generations of females

were told in order to progress in the corporate world, I thought I needed to be very aggressive as a leader early on, but it just never really fit me. It was never who I was. To me, this industry is really about the solutions that keep talent happy, healthy, and content. That's foremost to me.

Many entrepreneurs start their businesses because they want to be different from leaders they've followed—people don't leave businesses; they leave people. They often leave the boss or the perception of the leadership of the organization. So, when you start your own organization and you have the ability and responsibility to decide what you want that organization to stand for, be sure you've thought it through for the right reason.

Entrepreneurs sometimes think they've got to behave in a certain way. They've got to be ruthless and fast-moving. They're caught up in building something to make a mark or to be sold, and they have a board and stockholders to report to, so they have to be driven by a bottom line. They forget that the beauty of owning your own organization is that you can make it what you want it to be. For me, that was to support people, to serve God, to grow caring leaders, and to make a difference in the community. Whether it's a client who needs help with human capital, or a team member learning to use their skills for helping their family to make a financial impact (instead of only volunteer opportunities), PZI is about supporting people.

Sure, there are days when even I would like to call it quits. But too many others are counting on me and my leadership team. When I first started the company, making millions of dollars never crossed my mind. Back then, I looked to others to help me better understand how to start a company, how to make a profit, and how to develop people. But Michelle Nash, whom I mentioned earlier, often reminds me that I know our profit is in our people. Whenever I have income, it doesn't go in my pocket; it goes back into the organization for more staff, bigger offices, and more tools. The organization's success has allowed me to live my faith out loud and not apologize for it, and it even opens doors. That has come from leading with heart and being focused on supporting others.

When entrepreneurs struggle, it's often because of their leadership attitude and because they are not being their authentic self. They are not being true to their mission, and their leadership attitude may be someone else's instead of their own. Perhaps, their mission is not aligned with the goals of the organization that they created. Their team may not have the skills they need to accomplish that vision and to accomplish the goals. They may even have forgotten why they went into business in the first place.

Most entrepreneurs have a goal, and they see the fulfillment of that goal as their mission. My goal is pretty simple: *We Support People.* My mission is to support people to accomplish their goals, whatever those goals might be, and to be able to fulfill that mission by utilizing the skills, the talent, and the mechanics of the people that we have.

Decisions from the Heart

I've been a CPA for more than twenty-five years. So, I let my team know I lead with vision and determination, but I make logical decisions with my head, with my critical energy behaviors. I want to understand the hard facts—how things should work, what's logical, makes the most sense? But just because something is more logical doesn't mean that it's the right thing to do. Mark has always told our sons a simple truth, "The world will tell you that the easy decision to do is the right thing and the harder decision is the wrong one. But that is not true. The right decision is always the harder one to accomplish and will most likely be the unpopular and sometimes the illogical decision." That is so true in business as well. I cannot count the times that the right, tougher decision was not made because it was the unpopular one and no one wanted to make an "unpopular" decision.

When you're in the human capital business, leading often comes from the softer stuff—the heart. That means that, even when something doesn't seem logical, but it feels right, you have to trust that it's still the right decision.

Because I lead with my head and my heart, I am someone who is very slow to make decisions—especially the difficult ones, the ones that are going to impact people. Even though something may make logical sense to do, when people are in the equation, I take a step back because I know the heart can be misleading. The scriptures tell us to be careful of our feelings because our heart will lie to us. So, I pray a lot, and then, when there are no other right answers and the answer is as clear as it can be, I know I've led with my heart, not just my head.

Making a Difference

It's all about making a difference in where you are. Over the course of my career, there were a lot of jobs that weren't what I really wanted to do, but I would always find a way to do more than my job description. People often asked me why I took on so much more responsibility than I had to—I did it because I wanted to make a difference in someone's life. That was really always my motivation, and I used the skill set that I was blessed with to facilitate that mission.

For instance, early in Mark's career, before I finished my degree and started my professional career, I served as an installation volunteer coordinator of about two hundred volunteers across fifteen different organizations within the military organization. We were in a remote location at a British base in Belgium with maybe three hundred service members and their families. The closest American support installation was two hours away, so there weren't any American support services, and the British military doesn't do things the same way as the Americans. This was when it was just Mark and me, before we had our sons. We were in need of a community center because there was nothing there to support the mission of taking care of the people. I was aware that there were a number of vacant housing units set aside for military families from the Belgium government sitting empty. Since it was a joint military operational base, the Belgium government managed the housing that the other nationalities assigned their personnel to live in. I thought since the US government was paying for vacant units, why not use one of these as the community center that we needed? We weren't going to reconfigure anything; we just redesigned four bedrooms and a kitchen and a family area into a childcare center and a support assistance loan closet. It was a self-help kind of food closet and kitchen supplies and a place where people could come together, meet, and watch movies. I've always believed that the good Lord says, "Ask and you will receive," so I asked for and was given the procurement.

People often ask how military families survive all the moves or what was our favorite or worst place. I like to answer that my favorite place is where I am right now; again, it's all about making a difference wherever you are.

It's the same when taking a directive from Jesus: How are you looking out for your fellow human being? What is your attitude toward them? How do you help make them better? That's something you can do in business as well. Jesus always asked us to do more: Just when we think we have accomplished what he asked, he pushes us to do a little more. I keep that in mind when working with my own staff, especially new staff who think they can't do something or who think they don't understand. I tell them I'm going to stretch them until they almost pop—we're not going to let you pop, I tell them, but we're going to get real close.

When I started this business, it was because I saw a need to support people. International employees working abroad were routinely calling me and my support group for career assistance. After having worked overseas for several years and then having a management change or other organizational change and no clear role to come back home to, they were unclear of what to do. While that wasn't really my corporate function's primary role, nor was it up to my team to find them a job, we would stop whatever we were doing and jump in to support them and the organization. We took it upon ourselves to get involved in their careers, in the talent management, and in how they were going to get home because those people needed our support and the organization needed our support to keep their talent. We were holding management's feet to the fire to make that happen.

A great example of this is when my IHR group spent two years helping to set up a huge project where thirty people were sent to another country to open a research and development operation. There was a lot of money involved, and everyone moving overseas sold their homes and took their families and moved. Then there was a downturn in business and a subsequent reduction in workforce—40 percent of the US corporate workforce was laid off, and subsequently, those expatriated individuals' jobs went away. While the leaders in the United States were panicked over what to do with the hundreds of people who were laid off in the States, no one even thought about those thirty people overseas, much less their families—until I asked about them. Then one of the vice presidents took the time to work with me to put in place a plan for them to stay in place for two years, while other plans were made for them to come back to work in a different division in the States.

The Changing Workplace

One aspect of creating a Christian-based culture in business is love yourself and loving your enemies yet insisting on accountability.

Employees want an employer who is invested in them and cares about them as individuals, cares to know their family, and will invest in their development and future. I have found that employees not only want accountability but also desire predictability and consistency when it comes to accountability. Inconsistent application of policies or standards of performance will destroy morale and ultimately harm the organization, as a whole.

There are five generations working alongside each other at PZI, and this is not an uncommon scenario for many other organizations. As a boomer, I've been in the workplace when a sixty- to seventy-hour workweek was expected, and as a CPA, I like structure, and I believe it's needed. I'm old school. If you think about it, even though Jesus was a rebel, he wasn't loosey-goosey—there was definitely structure in the laws given down to Moses. He said, "I didn't come here to break the laws, but to show you that the laws are the laws of man." He was very stringent about his beliefs, knew his mission, and then carried it out. What better to do in business than to be structured, know your mission, and then fulfill it?

Younger generations, however, have many demands from organizations when it comes to the number of hours worked and structure. But the reality is, if there's no profit, you can't pay people. I don't mind telling my team members that, if we don't do our job and our clients leave, there's no money; if there's no money, you have no salary. It's just that simple. The money has to come from somewhere.

When I worked for large corporations, I went twenty years and spent millions of dollars as a corporate-level function, but that concept of understanding where the money really comes from was never really explained to me. While I knew my department didn't bring in any funding, I knew we were to be good stewards of the corporation's funding and to ensure compliance. But today, we have gone even further from that needing to understand where the funding is coming from to instead focusing on self-interest: How much money I'm going to make, what is my salary, what is my compensation package? Team members don't always understand the bigger picture: where the money comes from or the organization's mission. They don't understand that, if they help the organization grow, some of that growth comes back to them in way of a paycheck, bonuses, promotions, and incentives, and they don't always realize that all that equates to putting people first.

As organizations, we all talk about "people first," and "we care about our people, they're the most important part to us." Yet every organization doesn't demonstrate that. I wanted to bring a more collaborative, caring work environment into place while still having interesting work to do and allowing people to grow professionally and personally. My long-term mission is that, as PZI grows, its team members will benefit from that growth, from the fruit of their labor. I believe that if team members are being asked to do something above and beyond their job description, then there should be some long-term incentive plan to pay them to stay. But they have to know that the money comes from other people, the customers, the ones actually signing the paycheck—and that means people come first.

Even with Heart, Anything Can Happen

When I talk about leading with heart, I'm not proposing a workplace where anything goes. Yes, God is doing the driving here, but we've got our eyes on him and letting him tell us where to go. As long as we stay focused and don't waver, amazing things keep happening. My "intuition/gut feeling" is just Jesus talking, and I've learned to listen. But when that focus wanes, bad things can happen, even if working with a team with heart.

In one instance, a key individual was approached by another organization, and losing her would have been devastating to the company. She had been doing a phenomenal job, but without a title, others simply did not follow her—regardless of the role she held in the company. So I had to recognize that sometimes you have to ensure you give people the title and recognition in order for others to do the same. Fortunately, even though the other company offered more money, she chose to stay because she preferred the culture of PZI.

In another instance, I wasn't paying attention to logistics, and a large amount of funding was mismanaged by a member of the finance team. It was my own fault—I did not notice that the person was not leading in a godly fashion, excluded others, was secretive, and was not transparent. She didn't steal from the company, but she was just digging into accounts that she should not have, and we didn't find out until it was almost too late. I wondered why she was an unhappy person and seemed overwhelmed all the time, even with a team of five to help her. Turned out, it wasn't that she was overwhelmed; she didn't know how to do the job or ask for help.

When it happened, I went down on my knees and prayed to God to help us recover. I was also transparent with everyone in the company. I told everyone exactly what happened, took responsibility for the problem, and put some of my own assets up as collateral until we could recoup and recover. I never really thought about it when we were going through it, but those actions showed everyone in the company that I was in this for the long haul and that I could be the leader they wanted and needed. And by being transparent with them, they went out and brought in new business right away—for instance, Michelle, whose goal was to sell thirteen workshops, instead sold fifteen. By letting the team know the situation we were in, they were more than willing to jump with ideas and solutions to see us turn things around. It wasn't long before we won $15 million in new business. We call it a God thing, and I've seen it happen time and again. Since then, we've added significantly more people and seen amazing growth.

I've learned that if you are transparent and open with others, people either will or won't desire to work with you. I can gladly state that the individuals working at PZI prefer the transparency; in fact, one team member told me that a leader she worked for previously was very transparent, and she found it to be a very powerful way to lead. It has just never crossed my mind not to be transparent when it comes to my company. Starting a company is much like raising a child: You have to nurture it, be honest with it, and be willing to let it grow on its own. Besides, when you're transparent, you don't have to try to remember everything you're concealing from the team.

Patience and Prayer—the Path to Success

Years ago, in one of my corporate jobs, my salary was around $85,000 a year, and it always surprised me that the company would bill five times my salary for my time I put into a project. I used to think, "Why am I not getting some of that additional income?" But now, owning the business and seeing how the money really works and what it takes to run the operations, in people, supplies, marketing, compliance, and so on, it's easy to understand why you would charge five times as much. Entrepreneurship isn't always about trying to get rich—far from it. It takes a long time and a lot of investment. Sure, some people are pros at it—they form and sell companies over and over and make millions of dollars doing it. But even though our revenue is now in the millions, sometimes I still don't draw a big salary. If a financial problem happens, I'm the one who's going to take the hit.

I've counseled plenty of clients that grow so fast that their infrastructure can't keep up. I've even warned them against doing it.

But we all do it. As entrepreneurs, we start off slow, as we're trying desperately to get business, and all of a sudden, boom! It happens. Then you realize you've got to have people, you've got to have offices, and you're spending money after money after money. But the money hasn't started coming in yet. How do you balance that?

If anyone ever tells you that starting a business is easy, just run— they are lying to you. It takes time, patience, and a lot of prayer. When I worked in corporate, clients came to meet with the company; I didn't really matter. I just happened to be Deborah E. McGee who worked there. They were coming to see the company brand. When I started PZI, people did know Deborah E. McGee, so I had to brand the company. I remember so many people saying, well, the company really is Deborah McGee. I struggled with that for a long time, thinking of my corporate days and where I wanted the company and my employees to be able to stand on their own. But what I have come to find out is that PZI and Deborah E. McGee are one and the same, not separate. It is my vision, my faith, and my courage, all backed up with my "Business Jesus," that leads the company and makes the impossible, possible.

Points to Ponder

1. In what ways are you being your authentic self with your team?

2. When you make decisions, are they from your head or from your heart? How do you know?

3. How does your "brand" demonstrate your authenticity?

Chapter 10

The Goal—to Emulate "Business Jesus" in the Workplace

But remember the Lord your God, for it is he who gives you the ability to produce wealth, and so confirms his covenant, which he swore to your ancestors, as it is today.

——— DEUTERONOMY 8:18 ———

I've seen Jesus do some miraculous things in my business. I see it every day in the people we support, the companies that flourish from seemingly nowhere. I am not afraid to say I am a Christian and I follow the teachings of Christ: thus, we lead our business as he would lead his teachings, supporting those we can every day, using our intelligence and resources for good outcomes.

However, it wasn't always that way. As a leader, the first inclination I see in myself and most leaders is to be a driver. For me, that was definitely true. Back in my corporate days, I designed the program, I hired the people, I designed the policies, found the suppliers—that was my intellectual capital. As more and more people were brought in, it still always had to be Deborah's way. I remember distinctly one young leader coming to me, asking me whether he could change the way we did something. In my arrogance, I said, "Well, walk me down the steps of how you're going to do it." Then, with every step he shared, I said, "I've done that, I've done that. I did all that two years ago, and it didn't work. Why do you think that would work for you?" He backed down and didn't even try. What I later realized was that, just because it didn't work for me doesn't mean it wouldn't work for him. He's not me. The process might have been the same, but maybe he would have tweaked one or two things and made it work. I stopped him from trying. It really saddens me that I did that as a leader, and so I try really hard never to do that again. Even if he had failed, he might have learned something really valuable from the failure. If he had turned it into a win, he would have grown as a leader.

Now it's about stepping back and letting others lead, letting them answer the questions because there are a lot of good ideas out there. The results of my own self-assessment showed me to be 99 percent a director leadership style, which is what I naturally do. So it's very hard for me to take that step back. In fact, a direct report recently brought a plan that he had invested a lot of time in. Unlike what I did in the past, even though I knew his idea might not really pan out, I initially kept my mouth shut and just listened. Then I said, "It's a good start; it's definitely a direction we can go." That allowed me to take that step back without immediately just blurting out, "Oh, that's not gonna work." But it can be very frustrating, too, until I remember that even though I may have done something one way, that doesn't mean it won't work another way.

That's the shift needed in your leadership attitude as a leader. Leadership training will tell you to staff to your weaknesses, but when you bring in people with strengths that you don't have, you also have to be willing to let them take those strengths and run with them. In fact, the caliber of people who come to work for PZI blows me away.

This is a small company, and I can't always pay individuals the salary they are used to getting, but they want to work here. They want to be part of this. We have great leaders in this organization, and they bring such strength to the entire group. As the leader, you don't always have to be the one getting the recognition—at least in PZI, it's not that way. There's only one person getting the glory in this company, and it's not Deborah E. McGee. Who I am today is not who I was in the corporate world, but I still have miles to go to emulate what it means to be "Business Jesus" in the workplace.

Emulate "Business Jesus"—My Ultimate Goal

I've been talking my "Business Jesus" throughout the book, and maybe you noticed him on the cover. My internal perception of "Business Jesus" has long hair, a radiant smile, and an inner peace and knowledge. I know he's got my back, and everyone wants to be around him. He's one of those leaders who gets up on the stage and people just stop and listen to him. He really cares and shows it in everything he does, so others naturally want to be around that and emulate it. To me, that is what I mean when I say "Business Jesus." If you are a Christian and carry Jesus in your heart, then he is everywhere you are. If you are in academia, then he's Lecture Jesus; in medicine, then Doctor Jesus; in music, then even Rock Star Jesus (Jesus Christ Superstar). For me, it is in the business world, so it is Business Jesus.

When I think of Business Jesus being with me in every decision, being my "chairman of the board," I don't think of him in a flowing white robe on a mountaintop out of my reach but, rather, sitting right beside me at the board table, walking me through thoughts of "How are we supporting people with this decision? How will it affect others? Will we be better for this decision?"

As the CEO, I am faced with the difficult decisions, often ones that only I can make—no one else. That's when I know he is talking to me—in my prayers, my concentration, and my occasional one o'clock "business meetings" at night with him. When I realize the difficult decisions that faithful leaders through the centuries have had to make, and always went to God first to pray for guidance in those decisions, that's when I really know I am not alone making those decisions. Instead, I have my "Business Jesus" right there with me in everything I do, knowing that he is there giving me strength and courage and helping me ward off the "naysayers" who often will advise a more "logical" decision versus the bold and faith-filled ones I have made over the years. I take the verse, "Ask and you shall receive," to heart. How it shows up and when it shows up is not in my control, but I have faith that it will.

It's a pretty awesome task to run a business (sometimes almost over-whelming). In fact, when I stop to think about what I've taken on, it can be terrifying. We're dealing with compensation and employment all over the globe and regulatory compliance in so many areas, states, and countries. We want to be sure everything is ticked and tied and correct. The executive leadership team may think I'm making rash decisions sometimes because they are not always privy to my inner thoughts. I'm a critical thinker when it comes to decision-making, so I become intro-verted in order to do this. However, I conduct a lot of research, often for months, in advance of decisions. But I'm also an extrovert, so I speak to think, but usually there's a lot happening in the background, most of which are prayer and inflection. I've had to let my leadership know more than once or twice that, when I speak, it may not always be a *decision* and that they should wait until I tell them it is a decision.

When I pray, I always pray for wisdom, strength, focus, and the ability to be a good steward. In my prayer journal, my prayers often read:

> Lord, help me to be wise and seek counsel in you. When you bring unusual opportunities my way, help me see they are from you and take them without question. Lord, I thank you for the abundance of love you show me and the wisdom you give me. Help me grow your business to your glory. Help me see you in everything you do and show others what you do for me. Help me glorify you in all my accomplishments, knowing they are made possible from you and only you.

I pray every morning, and it never fails that answers come to me from something I've read or listened to in my daily Bible readings that day.

"Business Jesus" in the Workplace

One such reading, from Luke 20, was all about the how the Sadducees were trying to trap Jesus in his words so that they could find fault and condemn him. It made me think about how this could apply in business and reminded me of business development meetings I've had many times, where I knew what the person on the other side of the table was after, but they wouldn't come out and ask. Instead, they would take the conversation down a road, fishing for possible answers rather than first listening to the words and then finding the answers from that.

Jesus stopped and listened to the questions. He didn't let anyone provoke him into saying something that would give him away or give them the ammunition they were looking for to go against him. If we could all be more like Jesus in business meetings and listen to what the other person is actually saying (using active listening skills) versus what we want them to be saying, we would all be better-off. We don't need to prove ourselves when we have Business Jesus with us. Allow him to do the listening, and he will speak through us. Put yourself to the side, and let him have the floor. Things will come out, and the meeting will take a different path than you may have thought. When Business Jesus is in charge, great things happen. When we try to put ourselves in charge, often, we end up chasing our tails instead of leading. This is a great example of active listening, which we try to not only use at PZI but also facilitate in many of our workshops. Be sure you are listening and repeating back to the person what you heard them say to ensure what you heard was actually what they said. The skill is an amazing one to learn, and when we think of how long that has been around, it is quite astounding how much we forget about what we've been taught and just go with our "feelings." Feelings can get you in trouble more often than not when it comes to communication.

In Luke 21:1–4, Jesus looked up, and he saw the rich putting their gifts into the temple treasury. He also saw a poor widow put in two very small copper coins. "Truly I tell you," he said, "this poor widow has put in more than all the others. All these people gave their gifts out of their wealth; but she out of her poverty put in all she had to live on." In business, often we get caught up in the perception of the "rich in credentials": What school did someone go to? What job title did they have or do they have now? What is their salary? What credentials have they accumulated? But often we miss this fact: Those without the schools, the credentials, the high salary may be working with you because they want to be there. They bring value to your organization because they believe in your mission, your vision, and want to be a part of it, as a team member with you. If we treat these people more like Jesus treated the widow, we would see their value is far greater than the pedigree we often value the most. The people who want to be there for the good of the organization sacrifice their time and resources for your organization. The ones who are already credentialed may be looking only to further their career or use your organization as a stepping block.

As leaders, it is our job to be in the spotlight and put ourselves first. Be proud of your accomplishments, but remember how you got there. We seldom get anywhere alone: colleagues, friends, family, and mentors help us along the way. The next time someone congratulates you for a job well done, thank them and then remember to let them know that you didn't do it alone. Be open-minded, patient, and tolerant, and watch to see where new ideas may lead.

When God Enters the Conversation

I can't really explain the success we have had at PZI. We have always had people who wanted to be part of something challenging and wanted to learn in a safe environment. We believe that everyone can make a difference in someone's life. It doesn't have to be a big difference; it can be something small; even the little things add up and make a difference in everything we do.

Yes, it's an organization with Christian values that people of the same values are drawn to, and although we don't shy away from that, we also don't proselytize either. It is a fine line. God gives us a brain and resources and expects us to be good stewards and bring things back to him. Every day, we choose to let go and let God in, let him lead, and it's made an impactful difference.

Even in business, you cannot be afraid to speak your truth. Don't be afraid to let God in. As soon as God enters the conversation, other people start listening and impactful things start happening—especially if you've had amazing opportunities come your way, maybe some you were not expecting. There really are no coincidences; things line up the way they're supposed to line up. From a Christian standpoint, I see it as they're lining up the way God wants them to line up. Too often, people see things are not lining up, and they try to put them in place exactly the way they think it should be. But we're here to help our brothers, sisters, and colleagues, and when we do that, impactful things just really start to happen. We're really all one big family, and that's the way God wants us to be in this organization too.

As I write this, we're moving into a much larger space, and frankly, it's a little scary. Having Jesus with you doesn't stop you from being scared; it just gives you the trust and the courage to put the fear behind you and to know that it's OK to take that step out into the unknown and trust that he is going to catch you. You may second-guess yourself, as I often do, but I know Jesus always has my back; he is always walking with me every step of the way. He expects me to use my skills that he's given me to do the work every single day and to let him come in and do what he does best, which is just make miracles happen.

Even in my organization, those who work here see that every single day with me. And they see me use that to lead. Prayer helps me every day, and knowing that Jesus is there helps with my optimism because I know it's not all on me. That can definitely be overwhelming and make anyone negative.

If you are willing to be vulnerable and transparent and speak honestly of how your faith has helped you through difficult decisions or difficult situations, that alone is a huge testimony to the power of your faith. Often people need to hear and see the results, not just the preaching of it. For those who have not had the unexplained happen in their lives yet, hearing that those miracles and the faith that you have in them often may be just the one thing that someone in your sphere of influence may need at that moment. Then step back and let God do the rest.

I'm not proponing being too bold about faith in an unwelcome workplace; as Christians, I think it's important not to be a zealot about certain things. But by changing your mindset, people may begin to see it manifest outwardly. Use what you do to support other people, to show people the light, love, and care. Just show others that you care about them as human beings.

Points to Ponder

1. How can you step back and let others lead? How do you recognize the good ideas from your team members?

2. In what ways have you considered showing others your faith in the workplace? How has your faith helped you through difficult decisions?

3. How have you shown yourself to be vulnerable to your team? What effect has that had on them, on their view of you?

Conclusion

When I was a new manager at KPMG and I attended new manager training, the senior partner at that time, Jeff Stein, told the group something I've never forgotten: "As a manager, you'll work long hours and work harder than you ever did before, but *you* must set your boundaries—don't expect the company to set them for you. The organization isn't a person, it's an insatiable machine, and the more you give it, the more it wants. As a manager, set your boundaries, adhere to them, communicate them to your team, and make your organization a better place to work."

That's great advice, not only for a manager getting started at a large company but also for an entrepreneur juggling a million tasks and solving a million problems as they try to get their new enterprise off the ground.

Yet, it can be difficult for leaders to be their authentic selves when they are so concerned about the bottom line; many equate that to doing everything they can to keep people in line. Leaders, especially entrepreneurs, are often doing something that may not have been done before, and there may not be a set road map to follow. So, how can anyone in business indulge in their passion while also putting their people first? They have to be bold and willing to take risk that most people would not. They have to be willing to put themselves out there, and, more often than not, it is the passion they bring to their product, service, or business that engages people to trust them and follow them.

When I started to step out in faith and proclaim that faith was pushing me forward and would sustain me, even when there were failures and disappointment and naysayers, that's when PZI began to grow. You need money, influence, contacts, and a great business plan before you even start this type of journey. Well, I had had money, influence, contacts, and lots of "great business plans" from other people and other places, but I never really owned it. Those plans weren't necessarily my vision, and I was doing it for a company that didn't hold the same values around human connections that I did. Until I did find that connection, I never truly flourished—I had to lose my corporate career to truly find my calling and what I was meant to do and wanted to do, which is to help others.

I learned early in my entrepreneurial track that I don't have all the answers, but I can take my passion for helping people, be vulnerable, and let those around me see the real me and not just the subject matter expert CPA with the answers to the questions. I found that I could combine my knowledge with my passion of supporting others to watch people grow in their roles and in their lives. That's the difference between working with me and PZI and working with a big corporation, without the heart, passion, and authenticity.

The growth and expansion we've seen and continue to see at PZI is astounding to me; it surpasses anything in my wildest imagination. I've always known that the most successful organizations are those that operate as a family and have trust in one another, and it gives me such happiness to see that the family at PZI truly has confidence, trust, and faith in their colleagues and their leadership. As a result, the strength I have gained in my faith and in my belief in delegating to others and watching them "take the wheel" has been so satisfying. I owe that all to my Business Jesus, who gives me the courage to say, "Yes, we can do that," and to step outside of my comfort zone, trusting that he has my back, my front, and my sides.

In changing my leadership attitude, I've learned more about managing people than I could ever have thought, even with thirty years of business experience. This journey has shown me that trusting in my faith, my family, and my colleagues is what makes great things possible. My purpose is simple now: continue to emulate Business Jesus in my day-to-day business surrounding and dealings, not only knowing that I will fail from time to time but also knowing that he and those who surround me in faith are there to continue to work with me, encourage me, and share my passion for supporting those we encounter in our business world. If I can support one person to grow in their faith, their authenticity, and be able to know that they are not alone but are surrounded by love and courage, then I have truly done my job.

Acknowledgments

To my fellow military spouses, active and retired: You have always been my sisters/brothers throughout most of my adult life. Seeing your inspirational, spiritual, and determined way of tackling life in some of the most difficult and stressful situations has made me the woman I am today. Your faith in God has always shown through because he was the one constant in many of our lives, no matter where we lived or worked or the situations we had to endure. While the rest of the world slept soundly at night, we were the ones standing by our soldiers, airmen, sailors, and marines, understanding that the mission must come first, and we accepted it with the grace that God affords us every day.

To Terry Bentley, former Methodist minister for Guntersville First Methodist Church, and his wife Diane: Your straightforward way of bringing God's message to me for many years helped my husband and I find our bearing and purpose in God after retirement from the military community. You are one of the main reasons we now call Alabama home. Your challenge for your entire congregation to delve into the Bible themselves and read through it, all in one year, was a catalyst for me picking up the book and carrying out that mission, even though I didn't really know, understand, or truly believe at first. Having your down-to-earth actionable way of utilizing God's presence, messages, and teaching in everyday life helped me to stop and "listen" to God rather than my constant "talking" to God.

Through this one act, I was able to develop an active, listening heart, a new skill that changed my life.

To my former employers and colleagues: After twenty years of watching both the good and the bad of employer behavior, I can only hope that I am embodying all the good that I have seen. Working globally has taught me tolerance with cultures, different languages, and different business etiquettes. What I now try to embed in PZI employees is not tolerance but active understanding of each other's differences. Differences should be embraced, but one difference may not be better than another. Open communication, with standards of integrity, loyalty, faith, and understanding, is the value we embrace at PZI. Thanks to all of you who have helped to instill that into me.

To my current employees and colleagues: You make me better every day. You hold me accountable, and I thank you for that. My goal is to ensure you feel you have a voice in your organization and can expect the values Christ taught of humility, servant leadership, communication, and blazing the unpaved path to be the constants at PZI.

About the Author

After thirteen years as a consultant with Big Four global accounting firms, and another decade in International Human Resources (IHR) and global mobility management roles within corporate headquarters of European and Asian-owned companies, Deborah E. McGee started PZI Group. From a single incubator space, PZI has grown to a family of seven entities that provide international human capital solutions ranging from international employment setup to payroll in multiple currencies, domestic and international relocation solutions, decision-making for global employee information, international benefit solutions for a multinational workforce, and retention and engagement solutions.

Partnering with corporate leadership and senior business line executives on business strategy, Deborah's expertise is in designing and implementing effective, cutting-edge, and compliant human capital solution strategies and operations that optimize talent for worldwide corporations.

In addition to developing a business of highly accomplished global subject matter experts like herself, Deborah also provides cutting-edge operational workforce development training and leadership coaching, all in pursuit of her ultimate goal—effectively serving those who manage a global workforce.

Printed in the USA
CPSIA information can be obtained
at www.ICGtesting.com
JSHW021908190424
61528JS00001B/3